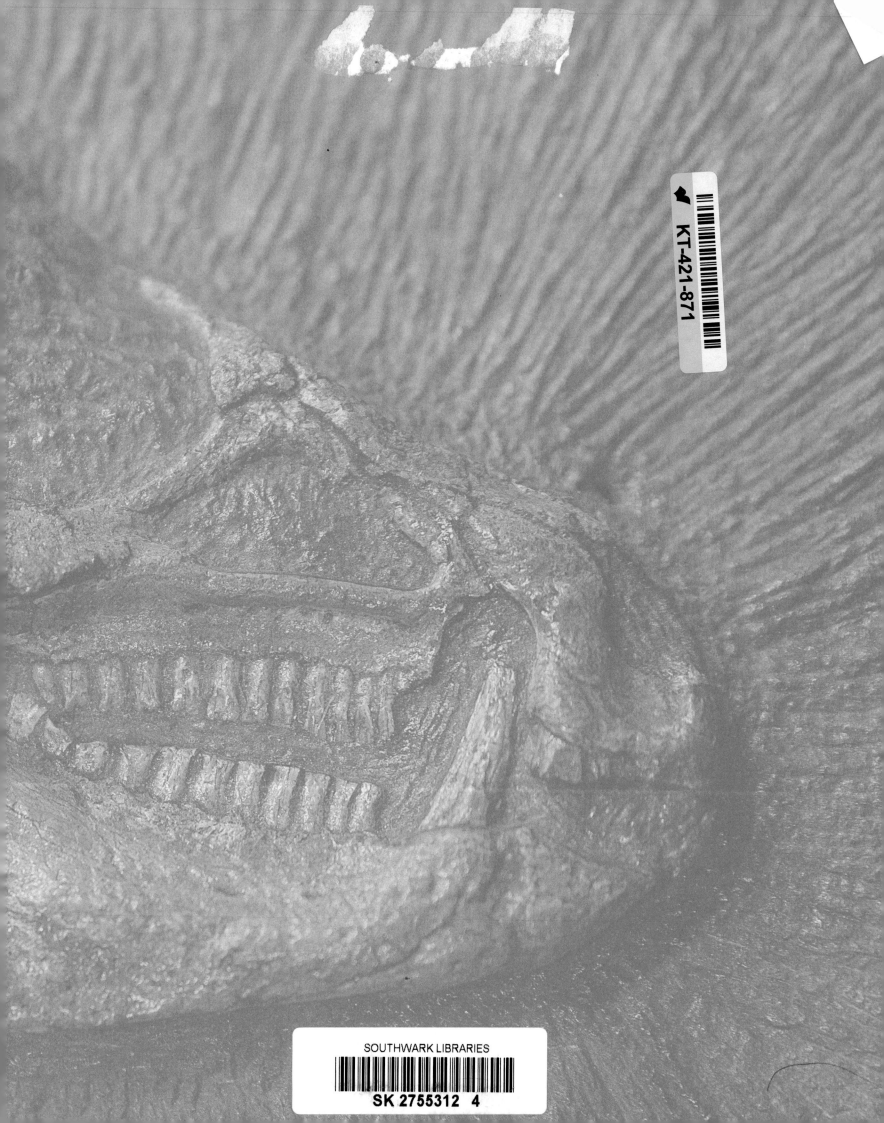

SUPER
DINOSAUR

SUPER
DINOSAUR

AUTHOR CHRIS BARKER
CONSULTANT DARREN NAISH

DK

CONTENTS

SCALE

The silhouettes in the book show you how big or small an animal was compared to the height of a human or the size of a human hand or foot.

Human = 1.8 m
(6 ft) tall

Hand = 16 cm
(6 in) long

Foot = 26.3 cm
(10 in) long

Penguin
Random
House

DK DELHI
Project Editor Neha Ruth Samuel
Project Art Editor Mansi Agrawal
Editors Kathakali Banerjee, Shambhavi Thatte
Art Editors Surbhi Bahl, Baibhav Parida
Senior Picture Researcher Surya Sankash Sarangi
Managing Editor Kingshuk Ghoshal
Managing Art Editor Govind Mittal
Picture Research Manager Taiyaba Khatoon
Senior DTP Designer Pawan Kumar
DTP Designer Mohd Rizwan
Pre-Production Manager Balwant Singh
Production Manager Pankaj Sharma
Jacket Designer Priyanka Bansal

DK LONDON
Project Editor Sam Kennedy
Senior Art Editor Sheila Collins
Managing Editor Francesca Baines
Managing Art Editor Philip Letsu
Illustrators Stuart Jackson-Carter, Andrew Kerr, James Kuether, Arran Lewis, Peter Minister, Simon Mumford
Production Editor Robert Dunn
Production Controllers Jude Crozier, Sian Cheung
Jacket Designer Surabhi Wadhwa-Gandhi
Jacket Design Development Manager Sophia MTT
Publisher Andrew Macintyre
Associate Publishing Director Liz Wheeler
Art Director Karen Self
Publishing Director Jonathan Metcalf

First published in Great Britain in 2020 by
Dorling Kindersley Limited
One Embassy Gardens, 8 Viaduct Gardens
London, SW11 7AY

Copyright © 2020 Dorling Kindersley Limited
A Penguin Random House Company
10 9 8 7 6 5 4 3 2 1
001–316686–Jul/2020

A CIP catalogue record for this book is available from the British Library.
ISBN: 978-0-2414-1286-2

Printed and bound in China

A WORLD OF IDEAS:
SEE ALL THERE IS TO KNOW

www.dk.com

WHAT IS PALEONTOLOGY?

Paleontology is the study of prehistoric life. It combines several fields, including geology (study of rocks), biology (study of living things), and chemistry (study of the basic building blocks of matter), to help piece together the evidence collected from fossils and the surrounding rocks. This evidence is usually incomplete because many important details are not preserved during the fossilization process. To make up for these gaps in information, paleontologists study fossils of similar species as well as modern-day animals to help them build a picture of prehistoric creatures and understand how they might have lived.

Paleontologists use small brushes and chisels to carefully uncover the fossils.

INTERPRETING FOSSILS

Scientists are frequently uncovering new information that changes their understanding of prehistoric animals. For example, for a long time a spiky bone found with the fossils of the herbivore *Iguanodon* was thought to be part of the dinosaur's nose. However, research later revealed that the spike was actually part of the creature's thumb. Paleontologists are constantly having to think again about their understanding of prehistoric creatures when new evidence such as this comes to light.

Thumb spike

BURIED BONES

Digging for fossils can be hard work. Teams of excavators sometimes have to endure tough conditions such as searing heat or freezing wind. This fossil hunt conducted by the Great Plains Dinosaur Museum and Field Station, Montana, USA, shows experts carefully chipping away at the rocks to reveal the bones of a large dinosaur.

The sediments brushed off from the bones are collected to check for small bits of fossils.

RECONSTRUCTION IN A MUSEUM

Some fossil remains are too rare or fragile to be displayed in museums. Skilled technicians make casts of these fossils out of lighter materials, which are then used to reconstruct the dinosaur like a giant three-dimensional puzzle, supported by a metal frame. These models, like the one seen here, are put on display in museums for the public, while the real fossils are stored safely behind the scenes for further research.

The positions of all remains are marked on a grid to help paleontologists work out what happened to the body during fossilization.

MAKING SENSE OF THE EVIDENCE

Taking fossils out of the ground and rebuilding them for scientists to study is not an easy task and involves several delicate stages. Skilled experts use different tools and techniques to compile the clues that can be found in fossils.

Preparation

First, the rock is cleaned away from the surface of the fossil using delicate drills. This process can take paleontologists thousands of hours.

Scanning the bones

In order to avoid damaging the fossil, researchers study the insides of the bones using powerful scanners.

Filling the gaps

Computer analysis of fossils allows paleontologists to study a find in detail, digitally reconstruct the missing parts, and work out how to repair it.

Creating 3D models

Experts create and print models of the fossils, which allow scientists to examine the evidence without handling the actual specimen.

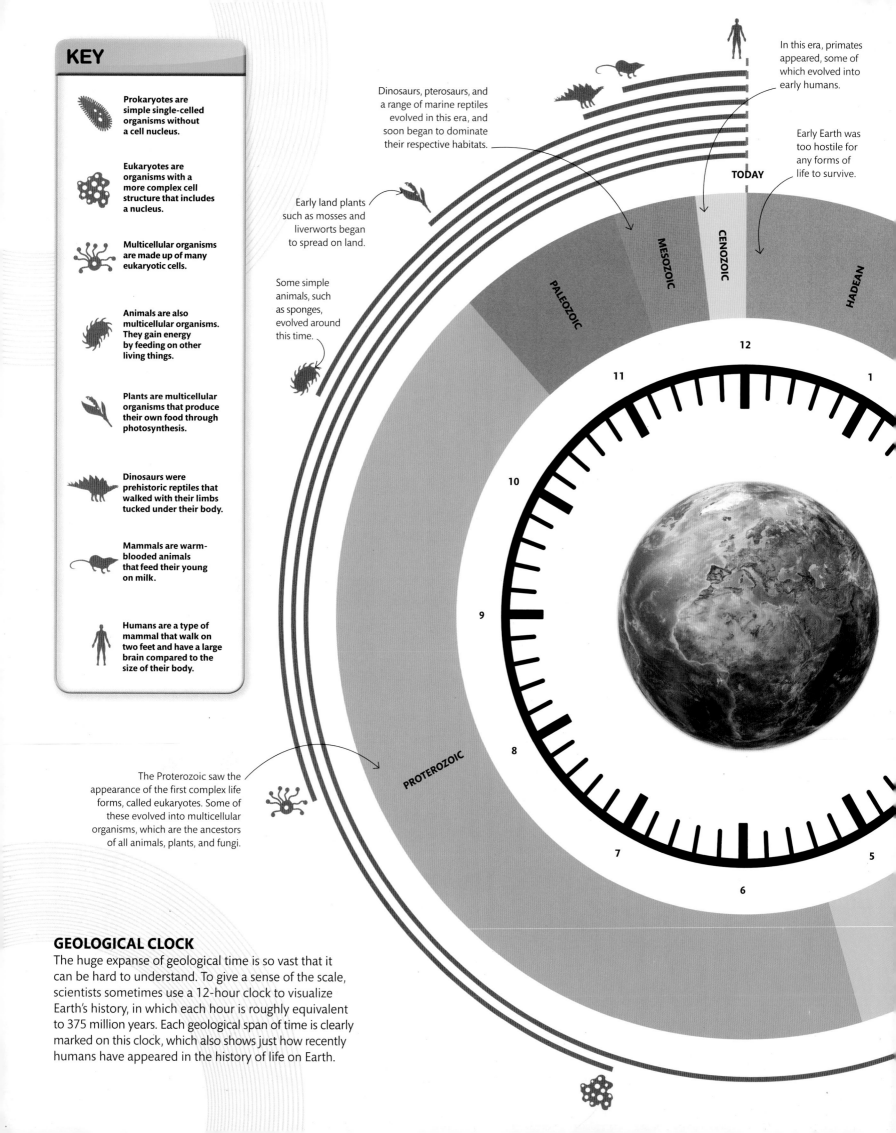

KEY

Prokaryotes are simple single-celled organisms without a cell nucleus.

Eukaryotes are organisms with a more complex cell structure that includes a nucleus.

Multicellular organisms are made up of many eukaryotic cells.

Animals are also multicellular organisms. They gain energy by feeding on other living things.

Plants are multicellular organisms that produce their own food through photosynthesis.

Dinosaurs were prehistoric reptiles that walked with their limbs tucked under their body.

Mammals are warm-blooded animals that feed their young on milk.

Humans are a type of mammal that walk on two feet and have a large brain compared to the size of their body.

In this era, primates appeared, some of which evolved into early humans.

Dinosaurs, pterosaurs, and a range of marine reptiles evolved in this era, and soon began to dominate their respective habitats.

Early Earth was too hostile for any forms of life to survive.

TODAY

Early land plants such as mosses and liverworts began to spread on land.

Some simple animals, such as sponges, evolved around this time.

PALEOZOIC

MESOZOIC

CENOZOIC

HADEAN

PROTEROZOIC

The Proterozoic saw the appearance of the first complex life forms, called eukaryotes. Some of these evolved into multicellular organisms, which are the ancestors of all animals, plants, and fungi.

12 1 5 6 7 8 9 10 11

GEOLOGICAL CLOCK

The huge expanse of geological time is so vast that it can be hard to understand. To give a sense of the scale, scientists sometimes use a 12-hour clock to visualize Earth's history, in which each hour is roughly equivalent to 375 million years. Each geological span of time is clearly marked on this clock, which also shows just how recently humans have appeared in the history of life on Earth.

HISTORY OF LIFE ON EARTH

Single-celled organisms, called prokaryotes, were the first forms of life to evolve on Earth.

Planet Earth formed about 4.5 billion years ago. Although scientists still debate about when life first evolved on Earth, many think that the first life forms may have appeared shortly after the oceans formed around 4 billion years ago. These organisms were tiny single-celled beings called prokaryotes. More complex organisms began to evolve a few billion years later, and these in turn evolved into the animals, plants, and fungi we see today. Although 99 per cent of all the life forms that have ever existed on Earth are now extinct, all known life forms, both fossil and living today, share an ancestry that can be traced back into deep time.

2

3

ARCHEAN

4

During the Archean, microorganisms such as cyanobacteria began producing their food by photosynthesis, a process in which carbon dioxide is converted to sugars, and oxygen is released.

THE ERAS IN THIS BOOK

PALEOZOIC (BEFORE THE DINOSAURS)

This era saw the evolution of a wide range of creatures, including fish and amphibians, as well as the emergence of the first reptiles and the primitive relatives of modern mammals. It is the longest of the eras featured in this book, and ended with a catastrophic mass extinction that destroyed 96 per cent of all species.

Brontoscorpio

MESOZOIC (AGE OF THE DINOSAURS)

Dinosaurs first appeared during the Mesozoic, which is divided into three distinct periods.

Triassic Period

The first dinosaurs were small, agile creatures. They co-existed with many larger types of animal until an extinction event at the end of the period wiped out most other life forms, allowing the dinosaurs to dominate on land.

Herrerasaurus

Jurassic Period

During the Jurassic, the dinosaurs ruled the land, and evolved into many large and fearsome forms. This period also saw the appearance of the first birds and some early mammals.

Stegosaurus

Cretaceous Period

Dinosaurs flourished in this period, which saw the evolution of many diverse species, and the appearance of flowering plants. At the end of this period, an asteroid impact wiped out most dinosaurs from the face of Earth, leading to the rise of mammals.

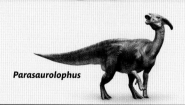

Parasaurolophus

CENOZOIC (AFTER THE DINOSAURS)

In this period, birds, the only dinosaurs to survive the end-Cretaceous extinction, dominated the skies, while mammals thrived on land. Early humans took their first steps.

Mammut borsoni

WHAT IS A DINOSAUR?

Dinosaurs are reptiles that evolved early in the Mesozoic Era, a period of time spanning from 252 to 66 million years ago. They belong to a larger group of animals called archosaurs, which also includes the crocodylians. All dinosaurs are vertebrates (animals with backbones), but they also share certain characteristics that are not seen in other animal groups. These unique traits help paleontologists to distinguish dinosaur fossils from those of other prehistoric animals. If an excavation reveals a bone or a partial skeleton that has one or more of the traits shown on these pages, it is very likely to be a dinosaur fossil.

FEATHERS

Recent research suggests that dinosaurs evolved feathers well before the appearance of the first birds. Many dinosaurs probably had feathers on their body, while some, such as this *Archaeopteryx*, even had feathered wings, which confirmed that birds evolved from dinosaurs.

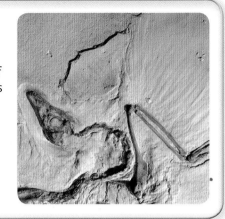

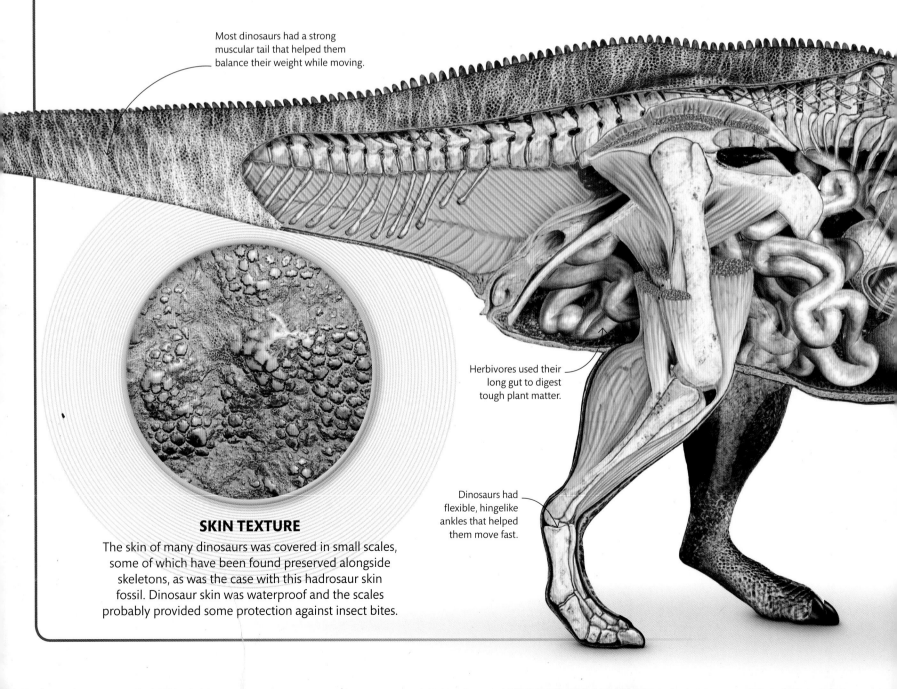

Most dinosaurs had a strong muscular tail that helped them balance their weight while moving.

Herbivores used their long gut to digest tough plant matter.

Dinosaurs had flexible, hingelike ankles that helped them move fast.

SKIN TEXTURE

The skin of many dinosaurs was covered in small scales, some of which have been found preserved alongside skeletons, as was the case with this hadrosaur skin fossil. Dinosaur skin was waterproof and the scales probably provided some protection against insect bites.

WALKING UPRIGHT

Fossil studies have revealed that one of the main features that distinguishes dinosaurs from other reptiles is their stance. Unlike most reptiles, whose limbs are spread out to the side, dinosaurs were able to walk upright with their limbs underneath their body.

Lizard
With their legs spread out, lizards have a sprawling stance that only allows short bursts of movement.

Crocodile
Crocodylians have flexible ankles that allow them to lift their bodies off the ground if they want to travel quickly on land.

Dinosaur
With their limbs tucked under their bodies, dinosaurs could stand upright and walk efficiently.

Inside a dinosaur

Although the internal organs of dinosaurs were often eaten by scavengers during decomposition, or destroyed during fossilization, some exquisitely preserved fossils do contain traces of a creature's insides. Scientists use these specimens and what they know about modern animals to reconstruct the internal anatomy of many dinosaurs.

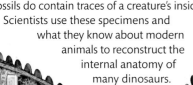
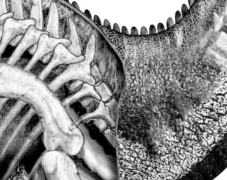

The beaks of many herbivores, such as this *Iguanodon*, had a tough keratin covering, like those of modern-day birds.

Dinosaurs probably had a powerful four-chambered heart, like mammals.

GROWTH TISSUES

When studied under a microscope, thin sections of dinosaur bones (seen below) reveal that these animals had tissues that helped them grow rapidly. Scientists think that dinosaurs probably grew at a brisk pace for several years before their growth slowed down as they got older.

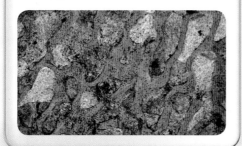

NOT A DINOSAUR

The Mesozoic Era saw a wide range of ancient reptiles flourish on land, in the air, and at sea. However, not all of these creatures were dinosaurs. Some, such as the pterosaurs, were cousins of the dinosaurs, but others were only distantly related to them.

Ichthyosaurs
These large, fishlike creatures were actually marine reptiles that gave birth to live young, just as modern-day mammals do.

Plesiosaurs
Instead of using a tail to swim, these long-necked reptiles used their paddle-like limbs to propel themselves swiftly through the water.

Crocodylomorphs
Relatives of modern crocodylians, creatures in this group evolved a range of different lifestyles and anatomies, with some reaching more than 10 m (33 ft) in length.

Pterosaurs
The first vertebrates to take to the skies, the pterosaurs had an elongated fourth finger, which supported a complex wing membrane.

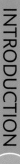

TYPES OF DINOSAUR

Dinosaurs first evolved around 245 million years ago, and spent the next several million years in the shadow of other land-living animals. It was only in the Late Triassic Period, about 225 million years ago, that dinosaurs began evolving into many different groups. In these early years, dinosaurs represented only a fraction of the animal population, but gradually came to dominate nearly all land-based ecosystems. Scientists think that dinosaurs might have flourished due to changes in the climate that may have contributed to the extinction of competitors. Dinosaurs are broadly divided into two main types, the saurischians and the ornithischians, which are each further divided into several diverse groups. However, some scientists have proposed the existence of another group, the Ornithoscelida, which is composed of theropods and ornithischians.

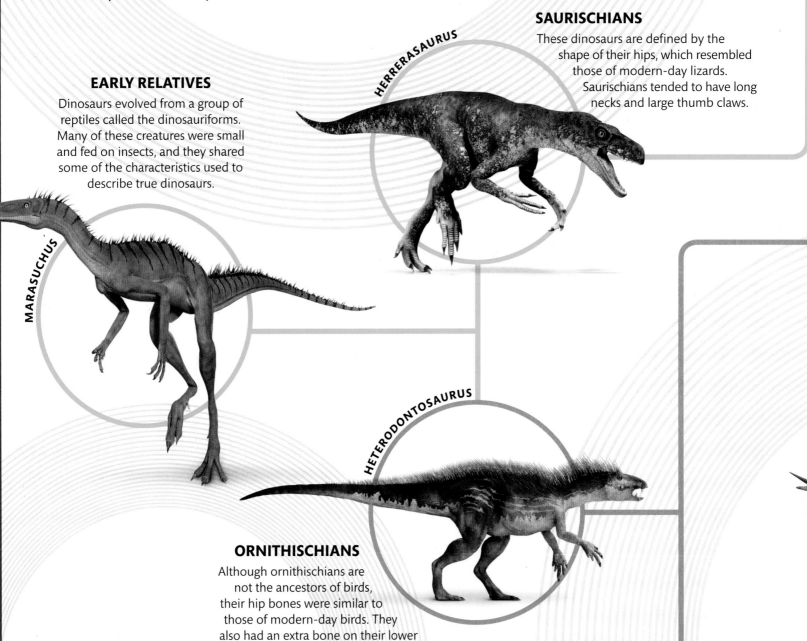

SAURISCHIANS
These dinosaurs are defined by the shape of their hips, which resembled those of modern-day lizards. Saurischians tended to have long necks and large thumb claws.

HERRERASAURUS

EARLY RELATIVES
Dinosaurs evolved from a group of reptiles called the dinosauriforms. Many of these creatures were small and fed on insects, and they shared some of the characteristics used to describe true dinosaurs.

MARASUCHUS

HETERODONTOSAURUS

ORNITHISCHIANS
Although ornithischians are not the ancestors of birds, their hip bones were similar to those of modern-day birds. They also had an extra bone on their lower jaw that supported a strong beak.

SAUROPODOMORPHS

With small heads perched upon long necks, these herbivores were the largest dinosaurs to walk the planet. Some that evolved later, such as *Argentinosaurus*, grew to record-breaking sizes – nearly seven times as large as an African elephant.

CERATOPSIANS

The plant-eating ceratopsians are instantly recognizable by their parrot-like beaks. In the Cretaceous, some forms evolved elaborate crests and horns, which were probably used to attract mates.

THEROPODS

The most diverse of the dinosaur groups, theropods gave rise to modern birds. Most theropods were carnivores, but some may have had a plant-based diet.

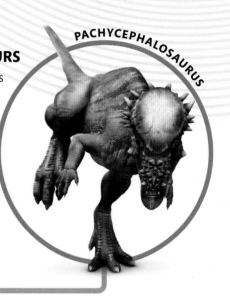

PACHYCEPHALOSAURS

These two-legged dinosaurs are easily identifiable by the extremely thick skulls that protected their brain from violent clashes when competing for mates or defending against predators.

STEGOSAURS

These generally mid-sized herbivores had rows of plates and spikes running along their backs. Only a few kinds of stegosaur were left by the Early Cretaceous Period.

ANKYLOSAURS

These stocky dinosaurs had wide bodies protected by extensive armour, and bony scales called osteoderms. Some later forms, such as *Euoplocephalus*, evolved large, bone-crushing tail clubs.

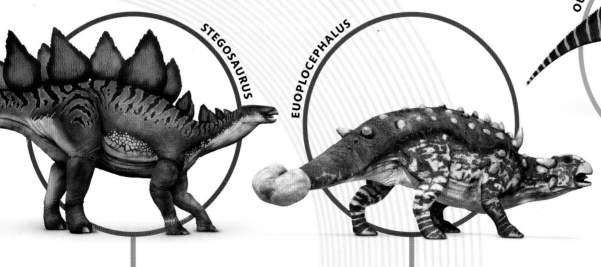

ORNITHOPODS

A large body and big nostrils were features of this group of plant-eating dinosaurs. Most experts think that they were social animals, and some even evolved flashy crests for display.

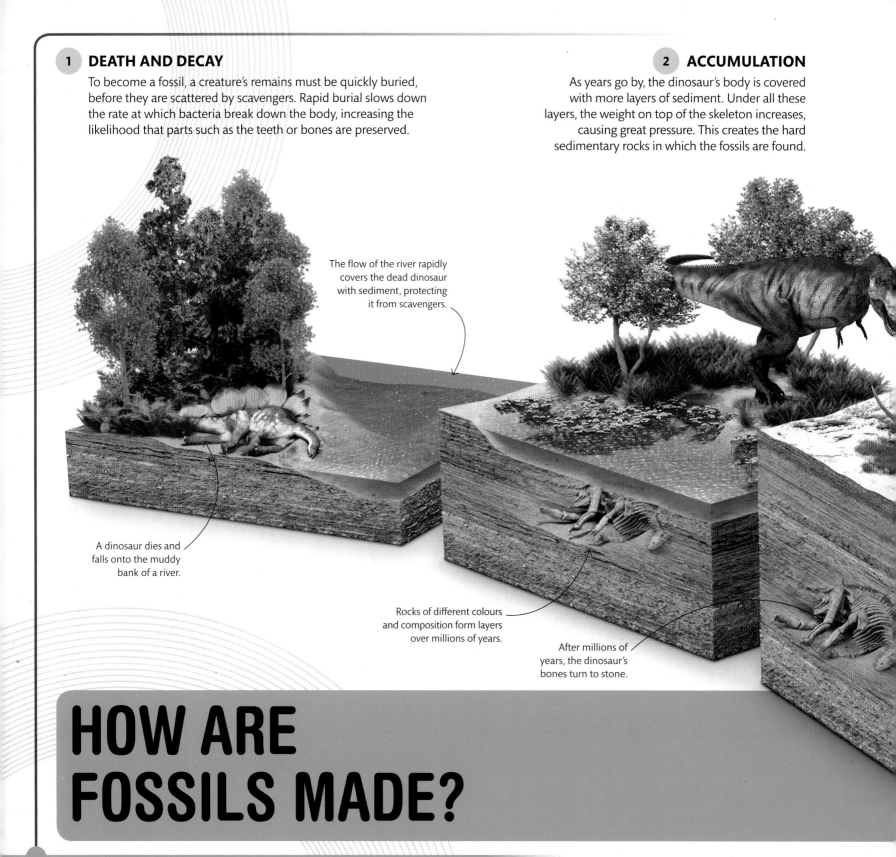

1 DEATH AND DECAY

To become a fossil, a creature's remains must be quickly buried, before they are scattered by scavengers. Rapid burial slows down the rate at which bacteria break down the body, increasing the likelihood that parts such as the teeth or bones are preserved.

2 ACCUMULATION

As years go by, the dinosaur's body is covered with more layers of sediment. Under all these layers, the weight on top of the skeleton increases, causing great pressure. This creates the hard sedimentary rocks in which the fossils are found.

The flow of the river rapidly covers the dead dinosaur with sediment, protecting it from scavengers.

A dinosaur dies and falls onto the muddy bank of a river.

Rocks of different colours and composition form layers over millions of years.

After millions of years, the dinosaur's bones turn to stone.

HOW ARE FOSSILS MADE?

A lot of what we know about prehistoric creatures comes from fossils. These are the remains of dead plants and animals that have been preserved inside rocks and minerals. However, fossils can only form in very specific circumstances, and most creatures leave no trace of their existence. Aquatic creatures or land animals that have been washed into a body of water and quickly covered by sediment are most likely to produce fossils. This is because they are protected from decomposition, erosion, and scavengers who might scatter an organism's remains. Large organisms with hard parts, such as a shell or a skeleton, also stand a good chance of producing fossils, as these tissues are more likely to survive the fossilization process.

BEFORE THE DINOSAURS

Dinosaurs lived during most of the Mesozoic Era, and the era before that is known as the Paleozoic. During this time, many wonderful and complex creatures evolved. Although several mass extinctions wiped out many species, some ancient groups of animals – including the ancestors of the dinosaurs – survived and even thrived.

Rigid, cone-shaped shell

Ambush hunter

Cameroceras hunted by ambushing its prey, grabbing its victims with its tentacles and pulling them up to its beaklike mouth, which could puncture shell and bone. *Cameroceras* probably preyed on armoured fish, such as the tadpole-shaped *Sacabambaspis* seen here, or other shelled creatures – including its own kind!

GIANT SHELL

AT A GLANCE

- **LENGTH** 7.5 m (24½ ft)
- **DIET** Carnivore
- **LIVED** 470–425 MYA
- **HABITAT** Oceans

Hidden at the base of *Cameroceras*'s tentacles was a beaklike mouth.

A smaller *Cameroceras* has fallen prey to a larger individual.

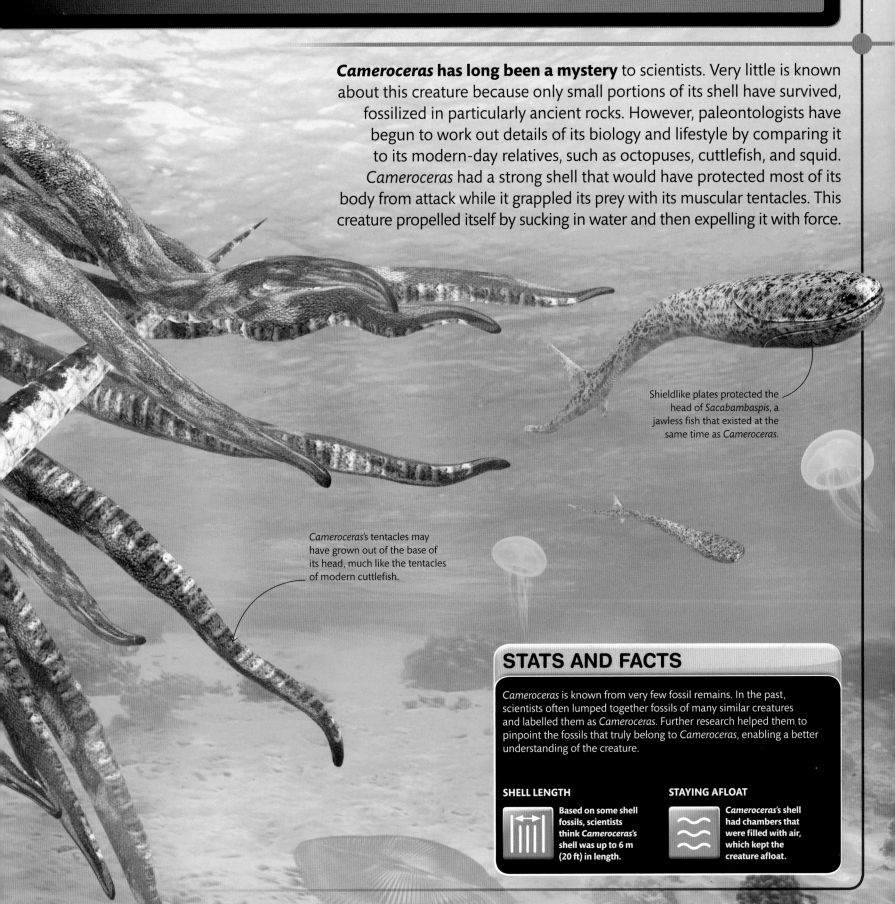

TENTACLED TERROR
CAMEROCERAS

Cameroceras **has long been a mystery** to scientists. Very little is known about this creature because only small portions of its shell have survived, fossilized in particularly ancient rocks. However, paleontologists have begun to work out details of its biology and lifestyle by comparing it to its modern-day relatives, such as octopuses, cuttlefish, and squid. *Cameroceras* had a strong shell that would have protected most of its body from attack while it grappled its prey with its muscular tentacles. This creature propelled itself by sucking in water and then expelling it with force.

Shieldlike plates protected the head of *Sacabambaspis*, a jawless fish that existed at the same time as *Cameroceras*.

Cameroceras's tentacles may have grown out of the base of its head, much like the tentacles of modern cuttlefish.

STATS AND FACTS

Cameroceras is known from very few fossil remains. In the past, scientists often lumped together fossils of many similar creatures and labelled them as *Cameroceras*. Further research helped them to pinpoint the fossils that truly belong to *Cameroceras*, enabling a better understanding of the creature.

SHELL LENGTH

Based on some shell fossils, scientists think *Cameroceras's* shell was up to 6 m (20 ft) in length.

STAYING AFLOAT

Cameroceras's shell had chambers that were filled with air, which kept the creature afloat.

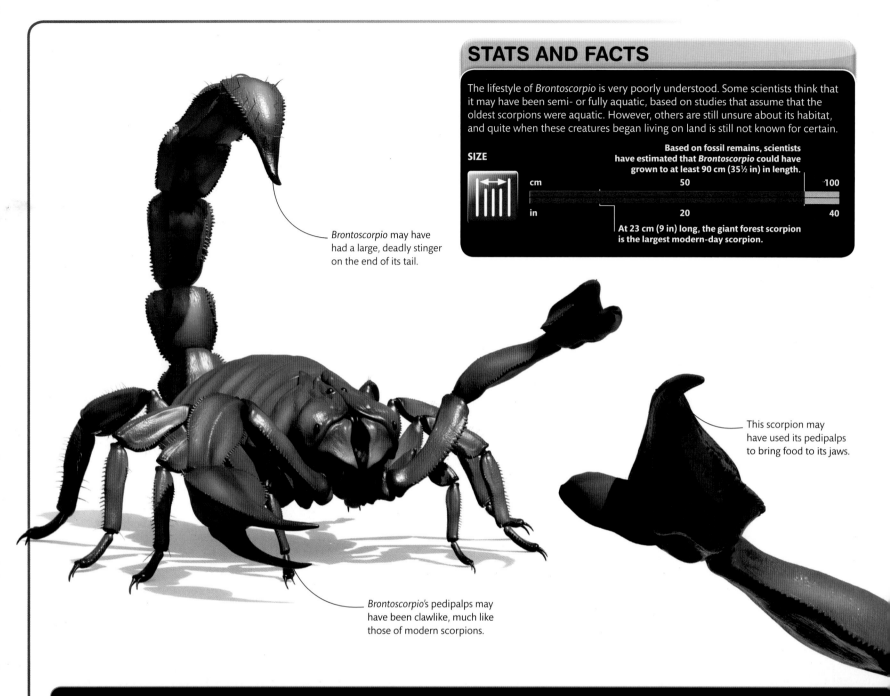

Brontoscorpio may have had a large, deadly stinger on the end of its tail.

STATS AND FACTS

The lifestyle of *Brontoscorpio* is very poorly understood. Some scientists think that it may have been semi- or fully aquatic, based on studies that assume that the oldest scorpions were aquatic. However, others are still unsure about its habitat, and quite when these creatures began living on land is still not known for certain.

SIZE

Based on fossil remains, scientists have estimated that *Brontoscorpio* could have grown to at least 90 cm (35½ in) in length.

cm	50	100
in	20	40

At 23 cm (9 in) long, the giant forest scorpion is the largest modern-day scorpion.

This scorpion may have used its pedipalps to bring food to its jaws.

Brontoscorpio's pedipalps may have been clawlike, much like those of modern scorpions.

GIANT STINGER
BRONTOSCORPIO

Despite being the largest scorpion to have ever lived, not much is known about *Brontoscorpio*, also referred to as "thunder scorpion". Only one fossil of this creature has been discovered, perhaps because it had no hard tissue such as teeth or bones anywhere on its body. This fossil consists of a portion of one of *Brontoscorpio*'s smaller "arms", called a pedipalp. However, its discovery has allowed paleontologists to estimate the size of this giant scorpion – it may have been almost five times the size of the largest scorpion alive today.

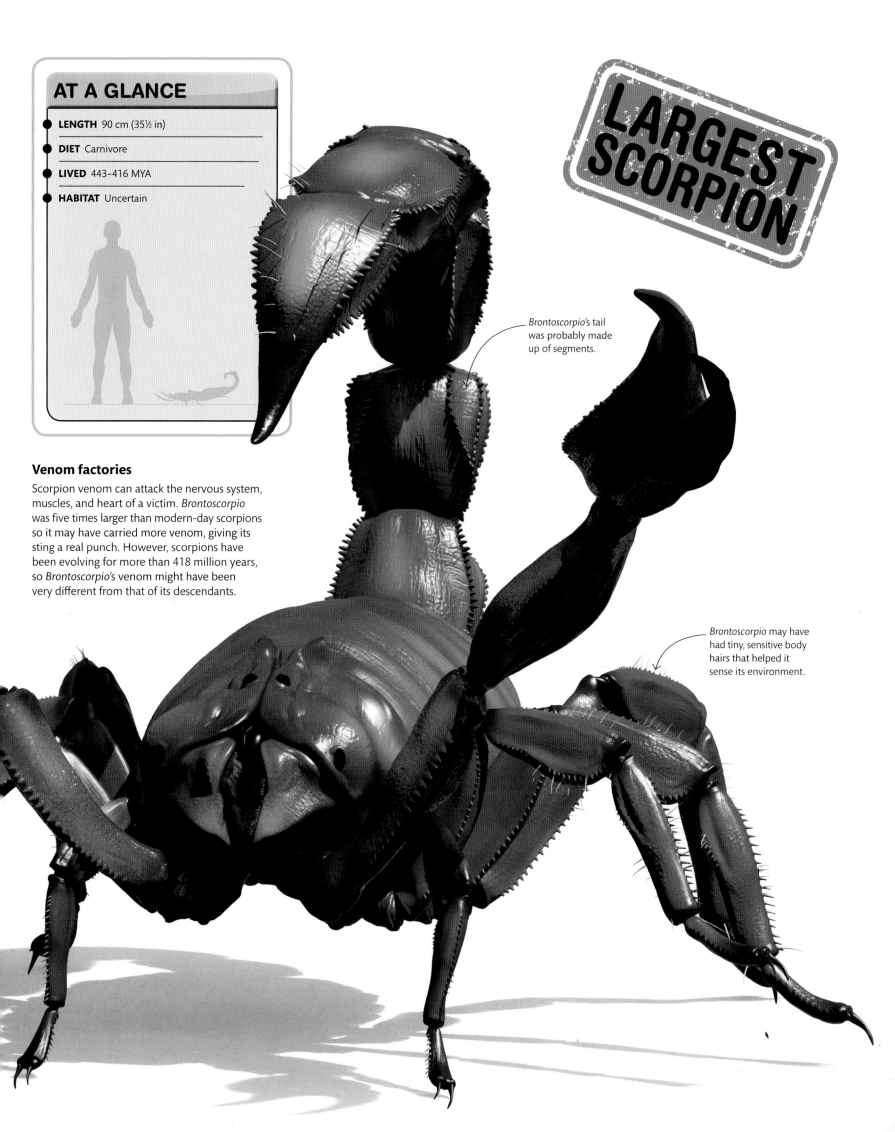

AT A GLANCE

- **LENGTH** 90 cm (35½ in)
- **DIET** Carnivore
- **LIVED** 443–416 MYA
- **HABITAT** Uncertain

Brontoscorpio's tail was probably made up of segments.

Venom factories

Scorpion venom can attack the nervous system, muscles, and heart of a victim. *Brontoscorpio* was five times larger than modern-day scorpions so it may have carried more venom, giving its sting a real punch. However, scorpions have been evolving for more than 418 million years, so *Brontoscorpio's* venom might have been very different from that of its descendants.

Brontoscorpio may have had tiny, sensitive body hairs that helped it sense its environment.

COLOSSAL CRAWLER
ARTHROPLEURA

This gigantic prehistoric arthropod (an invertebrate with a segmented body) was a relative of modern-day millipedes. Fossils of *Arthropleura* have been found in what is now North America and Scotland. At the time this creature lived, these regions were closer to the equator and covered in dense tropical forests. High levels of oxygen during the Carboniferous Period allowed *Arthropleura* to grow to huge sizes, unlike modern-day insects, which are much smaller due to the lower amount of oxygen in the atmosphere today. *Arthropleura*'s body is believed to have been made up of about 30 jointed segments, each covered by armoured plates. These plates were only a few millimetres thick, but the lack of large predators meant that *Arthropleura* was safe in its forest habitats.

AT A GLANCE

- **LENGTH** 2 m (6½ ft)
- **DIET** Living or rotting plant matter
- **LIVED** 315–299 MYA
- **HABITAT** Tropical forests

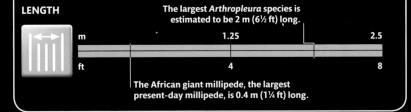

STATS AND FACTS

No complete fossils of *Arthropleura* have been found as the body armour of these arthropods fell apart after their death. Some partial fossils have been found, giving scientists a rough idea of *Arthropleura*'s possible size.

LENGTH

The largest *Arthropleura* species is estimated to be 2 m (6½ ft) long.

m		1.25		2.5
ft		4		8

The African giant millipede, the largest present-day millipede, is 0.4 m (1¼ ft) long.

CREEPING ALONG

The patter of *Arthropleura*'s many limbs would not have gone unnoticed as it scuttled about in the forest undergrowth. *Arthropleura*'s footprints formed large tracks up to 50 cm (19½ in) wide. These fossilized tracks gave paleontologists an idea of this arthropod's vast size.

ANCIENT ENIGMA

This fossil belongs to a creature called *Seymouria*. Although its large back bone and strong limbs suggested it might have been a land-dweller, research has shown that it began its life as an aquatic tadpole-like larva, just as modern amphibians do. However, it was not an amphibian, and was instead more closely related to modern-day reptiles and mammals. At 60 cm (24 in) in length, *Seymouria* was twice the size of today's goliath frog, the largest frog on Earth.

STUNNING SAIL
DIMETRODON

Although at first glance it looks like a dinosaur, this prehistoric animal was actually a different type of creature called a synapsid, which is more closely related to mammals. It appeared during the Permian Period, some 60 million years before the first dinosaurs, and may have been one of Earth's first large land predators. Fossils of different *Dimetrodon* species tell us that it was a fearsome carnivore. Its serrated teeth would have allowed it to easily slice through the skin and flesh of its prey. Scientists are unsure about the use of *Dimetrodon's* sail, but most think that it may have been used for display when competing for mates.

LARGEST SAIL: SYNAPSID

Dimetrodon's tail was made up of more than 50 bones.

Dimetrodon's short legs meant it was probably only capable of brief bursts of speed.

STATS AND FACTS

Dimetrodon had heterodont teeth, which means that its teeth had different shapes depending on their position in the mouth. This is unlike the teeth of most reptiles, but is similar to those of modern-day mammals.

WEIGHT

The largest *Dimetrodon* species probably weighed around 250 kg (550 lb), similar to a Bengal tiger.

SKULL SIZE

The biggest *Dimetrodon* skull ever found measures about 50 cm (19½ in) in length.

SAIL HEIGHT

1.5 M
(5 FT)

Heated debate

Dimetrodon's sail was supported by bony, rodlike extensions on its back. In the past, some scientists suggested that the sail would have increased the surface area of *Dimetrodon*'s body, allowing it to warm up faster under the sun. However, most paleontologists now consider this to be incorrect, and think that the sail was probably used to attract mates.

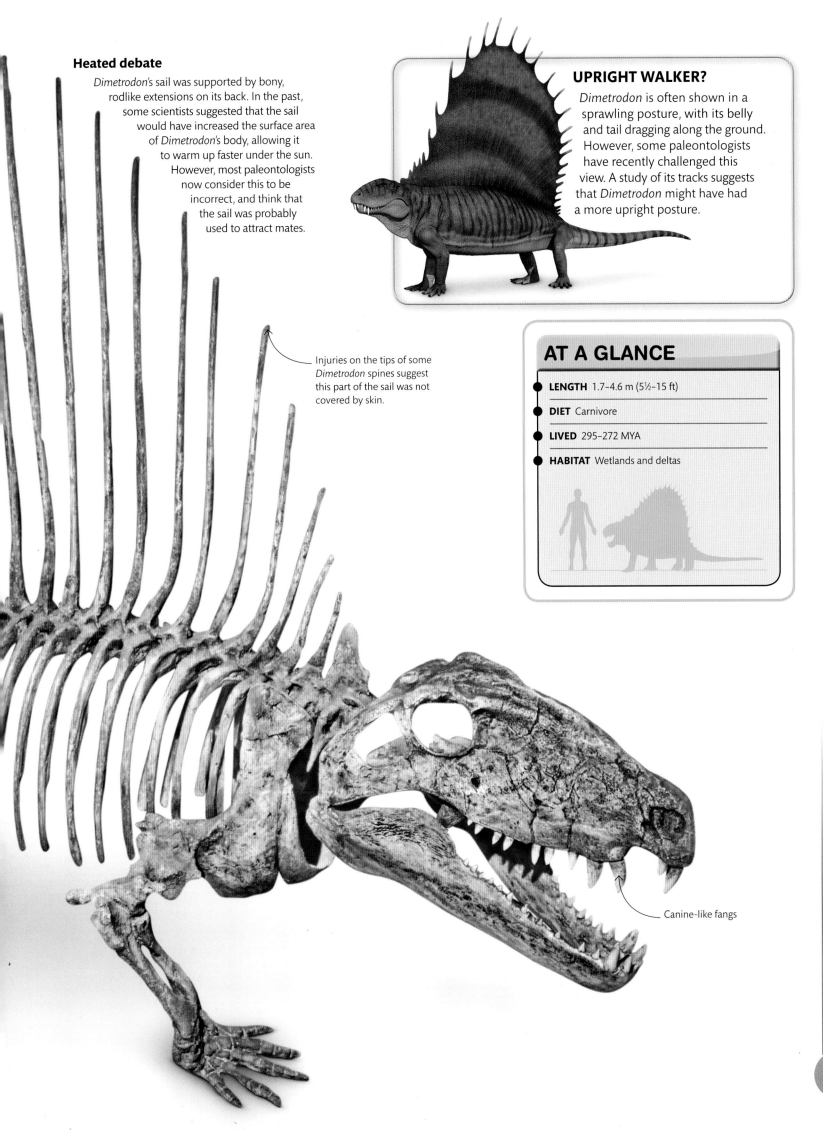

Injuries on the tips of some *Dimetrodon* spines suggest this part of the sail was not covered by skin.

UPRIGHT WALKER?

Dimetrodon is often shown in a sprawling posture, with its belly and tail dragging along the ground. However, some paleontologists have recently challenged this view. A study of its tracks suggests that *Dimetrodon* might have had a more upright posture.

AT A GLANCE

- **LENGTH** 1.7–4.6 m (5½–15 ft)
- **DIET** Carnivore
- **LIVED** 295–272 MYA
- **HABITAT** Wetlands and deltas

Canine-like fangs

Prionosuchus's 1.6-m (5-ft) long skull was twice the size of a modern-day gharial's.

AQUATIC PREDATOR

Prionosuchus's thigh bones were only 13 cm (5 in) long, which suggests that its legs may not have been much help on land. However, it had webbed feet, which when combined with a strong tail, would have allowed it to propel itself through the water with ease.

SWAMPLAND STALKER
PRIONOSUCHUS

With its long snout and sharp teeth, *Prionosuchus* resembles modern-day reptiles such as crocodiles, but it was in fact an amphibian. However, while most amphibians are adapted to live on land and in the water, *Prionosuchus* probably spent most of its time below the surface. *Prionosuchus* used its powerful tail to propel its large, streamlined body through the murky waterways of what is now South America. This deadly hunter was probably the top predator in its habitat, feeding on medium-sized fish, as well as primitive sharks, by rapidly swiping at them with its elongated jaws.

AT A GLANCE

LENGTH 9–10 m (30–33 ft)

DIET Carnivore

LIVED 299–272 MYA

HABITAT Swamps

STATS AND FACTS

Prionosuchus was initially only known from several fragments, which contained parts of a skull that was estimated to be just 50 cm (19½ in) long. It wasn't until a much larger jaw fragment was discovered that this amphibian's size could be properly estimated.

At 1.2 m (4 ft), the Chinese giant salamander is the longest amphibian alive today.

The 10-m (33-ft) long *Prionosuchus* was about eight times longer than the Chinese giant salamander.

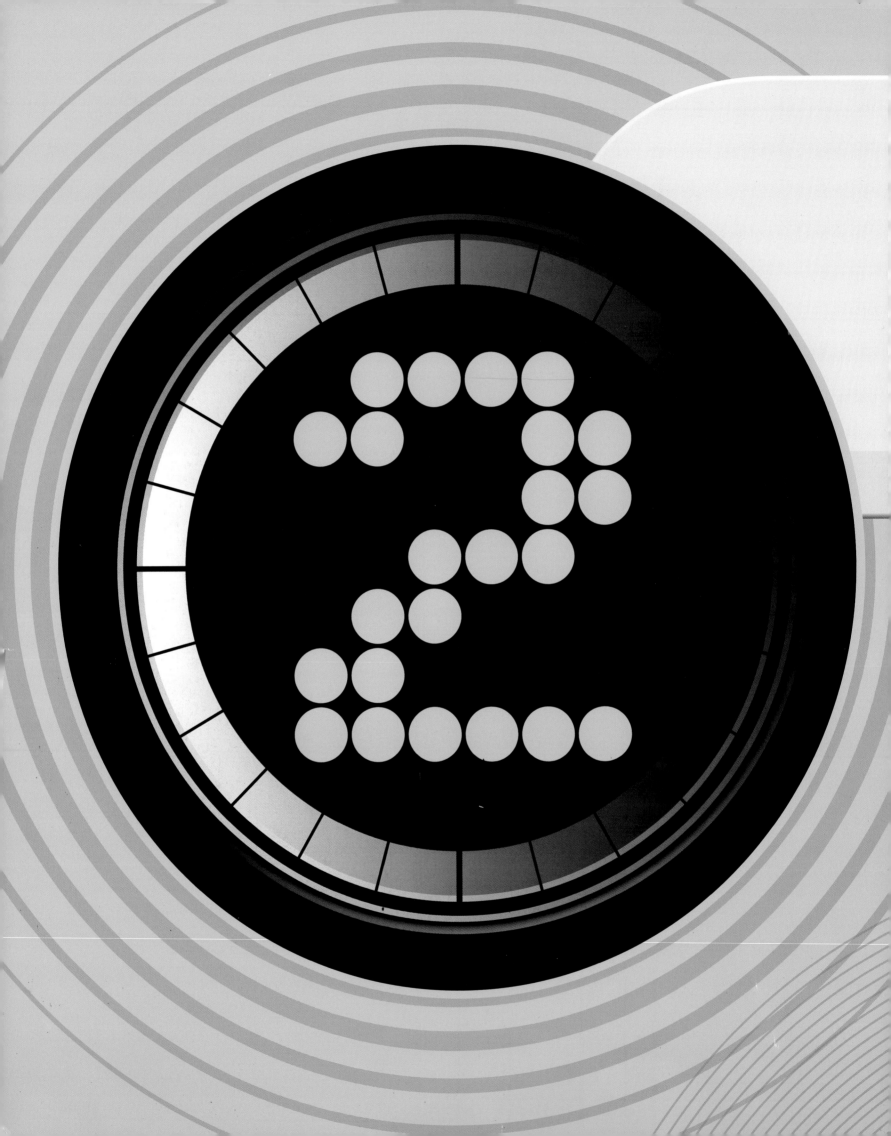

AGE OF THE DINOSAURS

Dinosaurs appeared early in the era known as the Mesozoic. These animals evolved into an incredible range of shapes and sizes. With some clever adaptations, they came to dominate nearly all land habitats, though they shared their world with many other kinds of animal.

STATS AND FACTS

While most early dinosaurs weighed up to 35 kg (77 lb), *Herrerasaurus* topped the scales at 260 kg (573 lb). However, it was not the largest predator at the time. That position was held by the land-based prehistoric relatives of crocodylians.

GRASPING FINGERS

Herrerasaurus had long, clawed fingers that may have helped it grasp prey.

SKULL LENGTH

The most complete skull found measures around 30 cm (12 in), but some may have grown larger.

Slender but well-muscled legs

Herrerasaurus was named after **Victorino Herrera**, **the farmer who first discovered its fossil.**

Long, pointed head

Theropod or not?

Herrerasaurus's position on the dinosaur family tree is uncertain. While it has usually been seen as a theropod due to its two-legged stance and sharp teeth, recent research suggests that *Herrerasaurus* may actually be more closely related to the long-necked herbivores called sauropods.

EARLY DINOSAUR

Herrerasaurus's long hands may have helped it capture prey.

Herrerasaurus's serrated teeth could slice through flesh.

PRIMITIVE PIONEER
HERRERASAURUS

One of the earliest dinosaurs to evolve, *Herrerasaurus* lived in the Late Triassic Period. It was probably a nimble carnivore that preyed on small prehistoric reptiles, mammals, or other early dinosaurs, and it had many features that would have made it a dangerous predator. Skull fossils show it had thin, serrated teeth and an unusually flexible lower jaw, which may have given it extra grip on struggling animals. *Herrerasaurus*'s long, sturdy tail allowed it to balance its weight over its hind legs, which may have helped it chase down unlucky prey.

TOOTHY ARRAY
HETERODONTOSAURUS

The unusual, turkey-sized *Heterodontosaurus* has confused scientists since it was discovered in 1962. Unlike the uniform teeth of most reptiles, *Heterodontosaurus* had striking, different-shaped teeth lining its jaws – an arrangement known as "heterodonty" – from which this dinosaur gets its name. This pattern of teeth resembles that of modern-day mammals, and has led paleontologists to believe that *Heterodontosaurus* had a varied diet – eating anything from small animals and insects to hard-to-chew plants. Paleontologists think its toothless beak as well as its long, strong arms and three grasping fingers, may have helped *Heterodontosaurus* grab its food.

SPECIAL TEETH

Heterodontosaurus's jaws housed three different types of teeth. The upper jaw had a pair of sharp tusks, while two unusually long teeth sat on the lower jaw. *Heterodontosaurus* also had short, cone-shaped front teeth and broad cheek teeth, which would have helped it grind up tough plant matter.

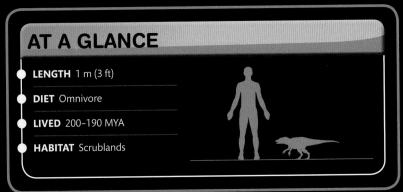

AT A GLANCE

- **LENGTH** 1 m (3 ft)
- **DIET** Omnivore
- **LIVED** 200–190 MYA
- **HABITAT** Scrublands

STATS AND FACTS

51 CM (20 IN)
MAXIMUM HEIGHT

Heterodontosaurus is known from some exquisitely preserved adult specimens as well as some rare fossils of youngsters. As a result we know quite a lot of detail about its lifestyle compared with some others from the Early Jurassic Period.

SPEED

Heterodontosaurus moved around on its hind legs, and could reach speeds of more than 4 km/h (2½ mph).

WEIGHT

Adults would have weighed around 10 kg (22 lb), with youngsters probably weighing around 2 kg (4 lb).

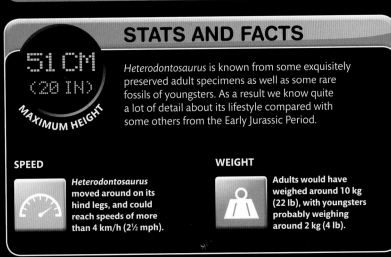

TERRIFIC
TEETH

STONY SKULL

This delicate *Heterodontosaurus* fossil was found lodged in hard rock in a streambed in South Africa. Paleontologists used high-energy X-rays to take detailed scans of the fossil, which revealed that the skull probably belonged to a young *Heterodontosaurus*, as its bones were not strongly fused together. Scientists then used the scans to make a full reconstruction of the fossil.

The animal's lashing tail might have been used as a weapon to defend against predators.

SPIKY SKIN
SCELIDOSAURUS

Scelidosaurus **was one of the earliest armoured dinosaurs**. It was a relatively small herbivore with a body covered in bony spikes. Low-lying plants provided tasty meals for *Scelidosaurus*, which used its small teeth and simple up-and-down movements of its jaws to break up and chew tough leaves and twigs. Although *Scelidosaurus* is well known from some magnificently preserved specimens, paleontologists aren't sure which dinosaur family *Scelidosaurus* belongs to. Most agree it is one of a group of armoured dinosaurs called thyreophorans, which includes the more famous stegosaurs and ankylosaurs.

AT A GLANCE

- **LENGTH** 4 m (13 ft)
- **DIET** Herbivore
- **LIVED** 199-190 MYA
- **HABITAT** Forests

Scelidosaurus's toes were tipped with blunt claws.

Multiple rows of bony scutes ran along *Scelidosaurus*'s back.

BONY DEFENCES

Scelidosaurus's back, sides, and tail were covered in scutes, which are hard, bony scales. Smaller scutes filled the spaces between the larger ones, allowing the skin to be tough, yet flexible. This light armour probably helped protect *Scelidosaurus* from predators without slowing it down.

STATS AND FACTS

Many *Scelidosaurus* fossils have been found in deposits containing lots of aquatic creatures. As it was not a water-dwelling dinosaur, paleontologists think that these individuals probably died near rivers and were then washed out to sea.

WEIGHT

Weighing 320 kg (705 lb), *Scelidosaurus* was light compared to similar creatures that evolved later.

SERRATED TEETH

Scelidosaurus had up to nine serrations on every tooth.

Scelidosaurus's forelimbs were sturdy enough to bear its heavy weight, suggesting it walked on all fours.

OUTSIZED EYES
TEMNODONTOSAURUS

The top predator of the Early Jurassic seas,
Temnodontosaurus was a type of large prehistoric marine reptile called an ichthyosaur. Its massive eyes may have helped it see in the dark, murky waters of the oceans, although specimens found in present-day Germany show that some *Temnodontosaurus* appear to have stayed near the water's surface. Along with excellent vision, this creature had large, sharp teeth, which it used to catch a variety of prey. While its diet mainly consisted of fish and other marine creatures, its fossils show that some of the species may have been able to catch and tear apart other marine reptiles, such as plesiosaurs and other ichthyosaurs. In fact, the bones of one unfortunate creature were discovered inside the stomach of a *Temnodontosaurus* fossil.

AT A GLANCE

- **LENGTH** Up to 15 m (49 ft)
- **LIVED** 198–185 MYA
- **DIET** Carnivore
- **HABITAT** Oceans

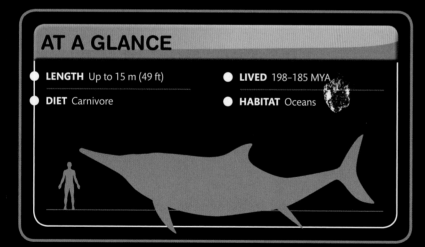

STATS AND FACTS

Different *Temnodontosaurus* species show varying skull shapes, which may have determined their diet. The long, thin skulls of some were adapted to catching squid and fish, while the short, deep skulls of others would have enabled them to attack larger marine reptiles.

LARGEST EYES

At 26.4 cm (10¼ in) wide, *Temnodontosaurus*'s eyes were even larger than those of modern-day giant squid.

CONICAL TEETH

Temnodontosaurus had conical teeth with ridges down the side, which helped it grip and pierce its prey while underwater.

ON THE HUNT

Temnodontosaurus probably used a technique called "ram-feeding" to catch food, opening its jaws wide as it swam rapidly towards its prey. It did not chew its food, instead biting off and swallowing chunks whole.

Gentle feeder

Despite its size, *Leedsichthys* mostly ate tiny marine organisms, such as microscopic zooplankton. Projections called gill rakers in its gills helped this creature feed in a manner similar to modern-day filter feeders, such as some sharks and whales. As *Leedsichthys* swam through the oceans, the gill rakers combed miniscule creatures out of the water, ready to be swallowed whole.

Fossils indicate that *Leedsichthys* had a large skull.

Large pectoral fins allowed *Leedsichthys* to swim efficiently and keep itself afloat.

GIANT FISH
LEEDSICHTHYS

The Jurassic waters were home to the massive *Leedsichthys*, the largest bony fish ever to swim in the ocean. This prehistoric fish was more than 10 times heavier than the ocean sunfish – the biggest bony fish alive today. Paleontologists have found only partial fossils of *Leedsichthys*, which makes it extremely difficult to calculate its precise size. Early research suggested that it may have rivalled the blue whale in length, but more recent findings have revealed that *Leedsichthys* was probably much smaller than the modern-day giant.

LARGEST BONY FISH

Leedsichthys had a toothless mouth, similar to modern filter-feeding sharks and whales.

AT A GLANCE

- **LENGTH** 11–16.5 m (36–54 ft)
- **DIET** Small marine animals
- **LIVED** 165–150 MYA
- **HABITAT** Oceans

STATS AND FACTS

45 YEARS OLD
OLDEST KNOWN INDIVIDUAL

Fossils suggest that *Leedsichthys* probably grew at a slow rate over several years. Even so, by the age of one, an individual would have reached a size of 1.6 m (5 ft). *Leedsichthys* was able to grow quickly in its first few years thanks to the rich food sources in Jurassic seas. Being so large from a young age would have kept it safe from predators.

WEIGHT

Scientists estimate that an adult *Leedsichthys* could have weighed up to 20 tonnes, more than twice the weight of a *T rex*.

GILL SIZE

One *Leedsichthys* fossil revealed gills over 1 m (3 ft) wide and 1.5 m (5 ft) long. Scientists think *Leedsichthys's* large gills would have helped it to take in enough oxygen for its large body.

SWEEPER FEEDER
BAROSAURUS

A gigantic plant-eater, *Barosaurus* was one of many large sauropods that lived on the plains of Late Jurassic North America. Early finds showed that it was roughly the same size as its more famous cousin *Diplodocus*. However, the discovery of a gigantic neck vertebra (bone) that may have belonged to a particularly large *Barosaurus* suggested that it could have been much larger. Paleontologists now think that some unusually large individuals may have developed enormous necks, measuring more than 9 m (30 ft) long. This elongated neck would have made *Barosaurus* stand out among its fellow sauropods.

Barosaurus's tail alone was made up of more than 80 vertebrae (bones).

SUPER LONG NECK

Some fossils of *Barosaurus*'s neck vertebrae are more than 1 m (3 ft) long.

Column-like limbs helped support the creature's massive bulk.

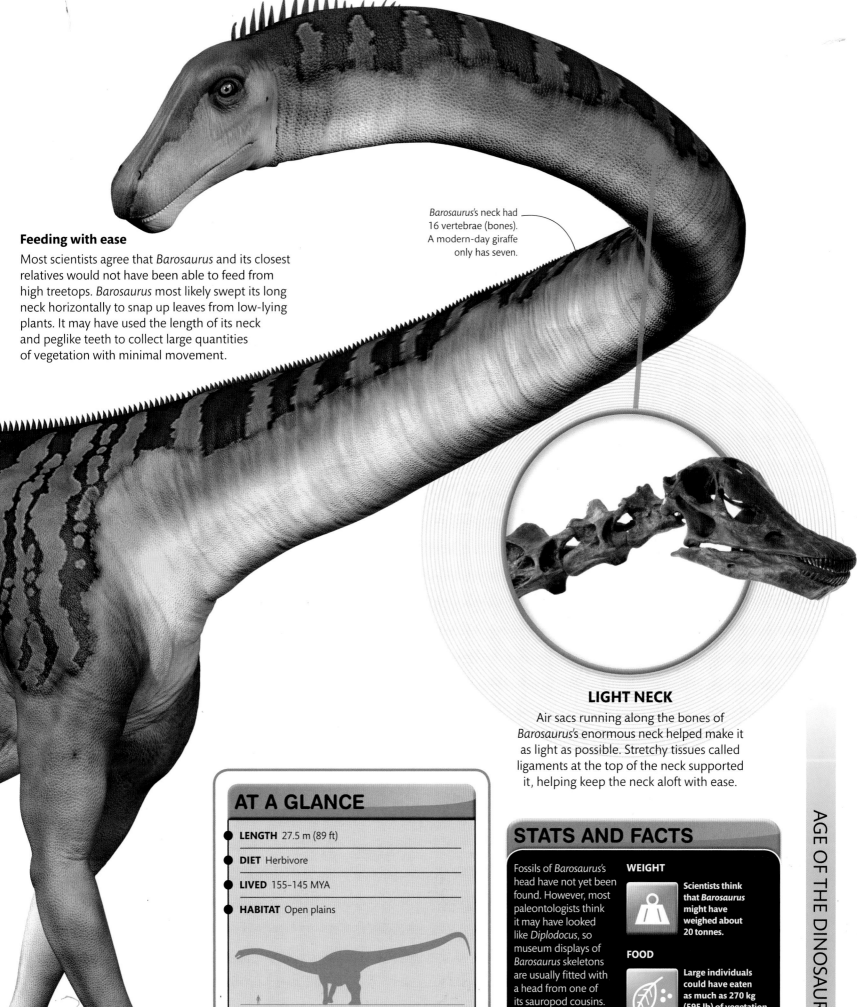

Feeding with ease

Most scientists agree that *Barosaurus* and its closest relatives would not have been able to feed from high treetops. *Barosaurus* most likely swept its long neck horizontally to snap up leaves from low-lying plants. It may have used the length of its neck and peglike teeth to collect large quantities of vegetation with minimal movement.

Barosaurus's neck had 16 vertebrae (bones). A modern-day giraffe only has seven.

LIGHT NECK

Air sacs running along the bones of *Barosaurus*'s enormous neck helped make it as light as possible. Stretchy tissues called ligaments at the top of the neck supported it, helping keep the neck aloft with ease.

AT A GLANCE

- **LENGTH** 27.5 m (89 ft)
- **DIET** Herbivore
- **LIVED** 155–145 MYA
- **HABITAT** Open plains

STATS AND FACTS

Fossils of *Barosaurus*'s head have not yet been found. However, most paleontologists think it may have looked like *Diplodocus*, so museum displays of *Barosaurus* skeletons are usually fitted with a head from one of its sauropod cousins.

WEIGHT

Scientists think that *Barosaurus* might have weighed about 20 tonnes.

FOOD

Large individuals could have eaten as much as 270 kg (595 lb) of vegetation in a single day.

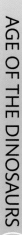

YOUNG HUNTER

A young *Tyrannosaurus* lingers behind a herd of *Alamosaurus*, looking to pick off an easy meal. However, these giant herbivores belong to a group of huge sauropods called titanosaurs that could grow to more than 25 m (82 ft) in length. Given the size of the *Alamosaurus*, the young *Tyrannosaurus* won't have much luck taking one down, and would be better off hunting for prey elsewhere.

FLASHY FEATHERS
EPIDEXIPTERYX

The tiny *Epidexipteryx* clambered around the Jurassic forests of what is now China on the hunt for its next meal. Its features and small frame were very different from those of a typical theropod. Its teeth, located at the front of its jaws, were angled forwards, and it had long tail feathers. What *Epidexipteryx* ate is still unknown, but its small size and pointy teeth lead paleontologists to believe that it probably preyed mainly on insects.

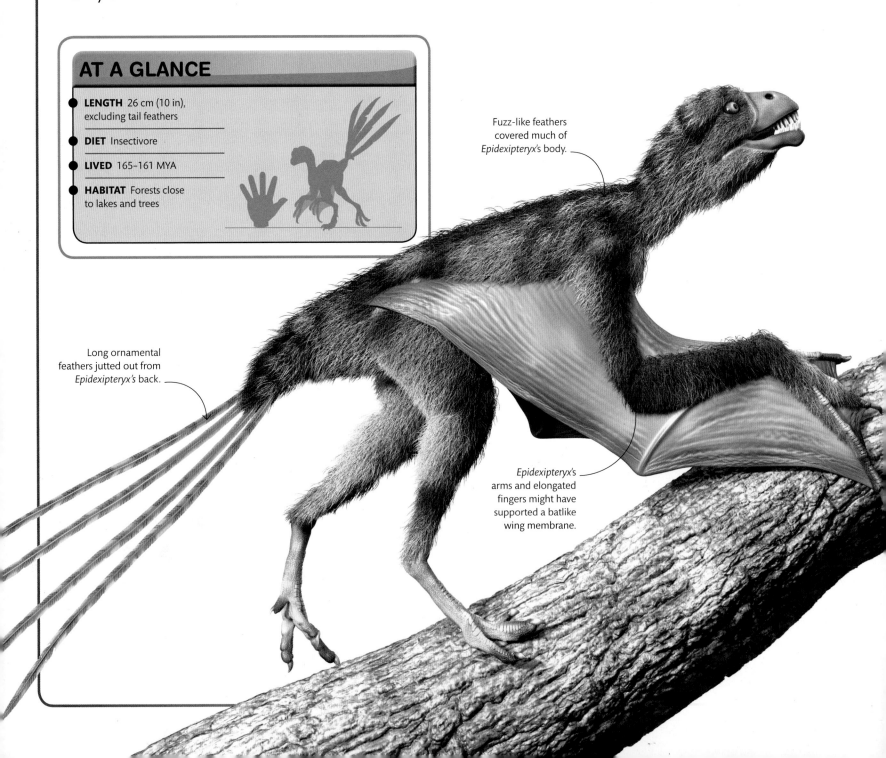

AT A GLANCE

- **LENGTH** 26 cm (10 in), excluding tail feathers
- **DIET** Insectivore
- **LIVED** 165–161 MYA
- **HABITAT** Forests close to lakes and trees

Fuzz-like feathers covered much of *Epidexipteryx*'s body.

Long ornamental feathers jutted out from *Epidexipteryx*'s back.

Epidexipteryx's arms and elongated fingers might have supported a batlike wing membrane.

The colour of *Epidexipteryx's* coat probably provided it with camouflage in its forest habitat.

Epidexipteryx's back legs may not have been covered with the fuzz-like feathers.

The animal's sharp teeth formed a scoop in the front of its mouth that helped it gather insects.

Elaborate displays

Epidexipteryx's four tail feathers were probably the same length as the creature's body. Given their size and number, and how similar they were to the display feathers of modern birds such as the peacock, they were probably used to impress mates.

STATS AND FACTS

Epidexipteryx is only known from the fossil of one specimen. Weighing around 164 g (6 oz), it was possibly one of the smallest dinosaurs ever. One small theropod that may have been lighter is *Parvicursor*.

TAIL FEATHERS

Epidexipteryx's fossil shows that its tail feathers were at least 19 cm (7½ in) long, and may have been brightly coloured.

TINY THIGH BONE

At about 5 cm (2 in) in length, *Epidexipteryx's* thigh bone was around half the size of that of a chicken.

Epidexipteryx is the **oldest known group** of animals to have ornamental tail feathers.

STRIKING PLATES
STEGOSAURUS

With a neck and back lined with a spectacular double row of plates, and a tail armed with four dangerous spikes, *Stegosaurus* was the largest of all the stegosaurs – a group of plant-eating dinosaurs with plates on their backs. The plates were bony structures, called osteoderms, which grew directly from the animal's skin. These were probably covered in tough keratin – the same material that forms the beaks of birds – and might have played a role in display. *Stegosaurus* is known from fossils found in what is now North America and Portugal, which suggests that a land bridge could have connected North America and Europe at the time.

Torvosaurus was one of the biggest predators during the Late Jurassic Period.

Stegosaurus would thrash its flexible tail about to ward off predators.

STATS AND FACTS

Stegosaurus had a strong skull and could bite down with a force of about 40 kg (88 lb), which is powerful for a herbivore. This would have allowed it to feed on a wide variety of tough vegetation.

TAIL SPIKES

The spikes on *Stegosaurus's* tail grew to a length of 1 m (3 in).

WEIGHT

Paleontologists estimate that the heaviest *Stegosaurus* could have weighed up to 7 tonnes.

Spiky defence

Stegosaurus may have used its tail in fights to defend itself from predators such as this *Torvosaurus*. Paleontologists have found fossils of several *Stegosaurus* tail spikes with damaged and infected tips. Fossils of the carnivorous *Allosaurus*, which lived at the same time, also show gruesome injuries that fit the shape of *Stegosaurus*'s spikes.

AT A GLANCE

- **LENGTH** 9 m (30 ft)
- **DIET** Herbivore
- **LIVED** 155–151 MYA
- **HABITAT** Forests

These large plates probably had more to do with attracting a mate than with defence.

MARINE MARAUDER
PLATYPTERYGIUS

One of the top marine hunters of its time, the deadly *Platypterygius* cruised the oceans preying on a variety of creatures with its large, conical teeth. It was a type of prehistoric sea-dwelling reptile called an ichthyosaur. While many ichthyosaurs had big flippers, fossils show that *Platypterygius* took this trait to the extreme: its front flippers had evolved to form large paddles that helped it steer through the water with ease. Paleontologists have discovered *Platypterygius* fossils in Cretaceous rocks in many different places, which suggests it may have been spread across several ancient seas.

MOST FINGER BONES

Scientists think that *Platypterygius* may have had a blubber-like layer of fat that kept it warm, like modern-day whales and leatherback turtles.

FISH-SHAPED REPTILE

Although not directly related to modern-day fish, ichthyosaurs, such as *Platypterygius*, had fishlike proportions and features that helped them survive in their aquatic habitat. For example, *Platypterygius*'s large tail generated enough thrust to propel its streamlined body through the water.

A ring of bone supported *Platypterygius*'s eyeball.

Modified hands

Attached to a small, bulky arm, *Platypterygius*'s large front flippers were modified hands, with about seven to nine fingers each. These fingers contained a large number of tiny bones that made the flippers rigid, allowing the creature to navigate efficiently through the water and keep itself afloat.

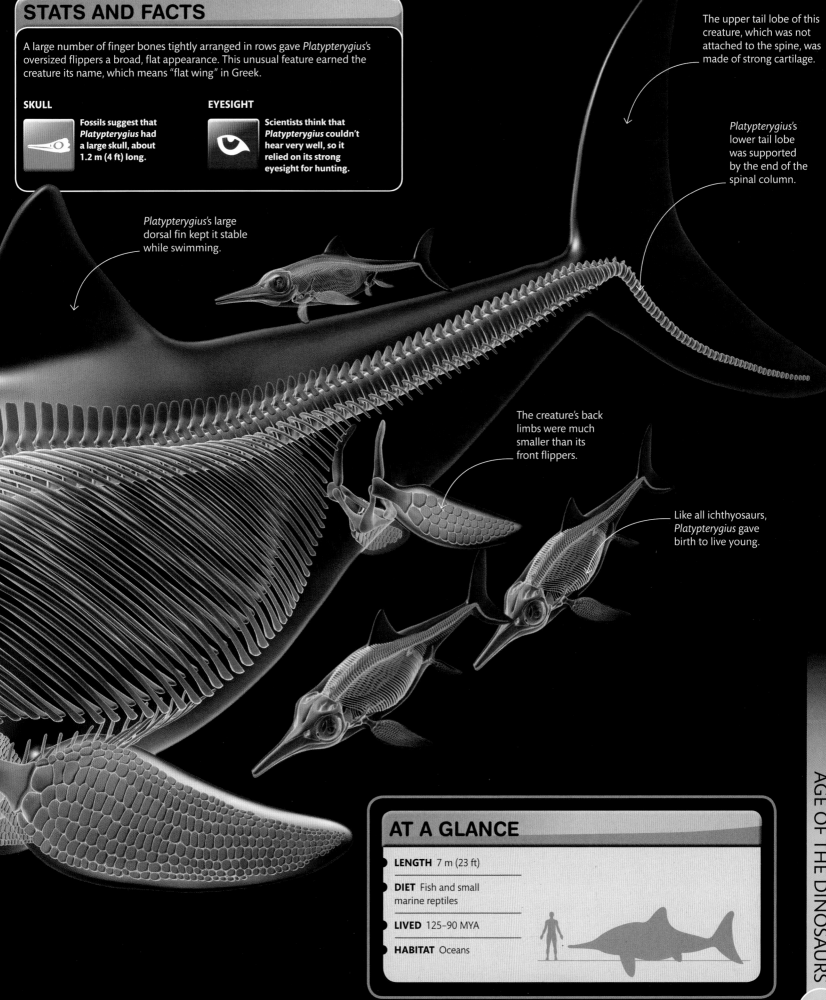

STATS AND FACTS

A large number of finger bones tightly arranged in rows gave *Platypterygius's* oversized flippers a broad, flat appearance. This unusual feature earned the creature its name, which means "flat wing" in Greek.

SKULL

Fossils suggest that *Platypterygius* had a large skull, about 1.2 m (4 ft) long.

EYESIGHT

Scientists think that *Platypterygius* couldn't hear very well, so it relied on its strong eyesight for hunting.

The upper tail lobe of this creature, which was not attached to the spine, was made of strong cartilage.

Platypterygius's lower tail lobe was supported by the end of the spinal column.

Platypterygius's large dorsal fin kept it stable while swimming.

The creature's back limbs were much smaller than its front flippers.

Like all ichthyosaurs, *Platypterygius* gave birth to live young.

AT A GLANCE

- **LENGTH** 7 m (23 ft)
- **DIET** Fish and small marine reptiles
- **LIVED** 125–90 MYA
- **HABITAT** Oceans

A small fluke on the tail may have helped *Pliosaurus* steer.

Pliosaurus used its large shoulder and chest muscles to power its front flippers as it scanned the oceans for food or rivals.

***Pliosaurus* could take down prey larger than a camper van.**

UNDERWATER KILLER
PLIOSAURUS

Very few competitors could challenge the formidable *Pliosaurus* as it patrolled the Jurassic seas in search of prey. Its immense skull housed the powerful jaws and teeth it needed to capture and consume the huge fish and marine reptiles that made up its diet. Research suggests that *Pliosaurus* probably used all four of its flippers as it swam, with each pair working together to propel the creature through the water.

STRONGEST BITE: MARINE REPTILE

STATS AND FACTS

The skull fossils of *Pliosaurus* were embedded in a rocky cliff off the coast of Dorset, England. They were exposed over time as the cliff face wore away, but even after they were uncovered, it took paleontologists almost eight years to collect them all.

SKULL LENGTH

The skull of *Pliosaurus* was 2 m (6½ ft) in length.

m		1.5		3
ft		5		10

The average height of a human male is 1.8 m (6 ft).

Dakosaurus, a smaller marine reptile, would have made a tasty meal for *Pliosaurus*.

Jaws of death

Only *Pliosaurus kevani*'s skull has been found. It contained bone-crushing jaws and teeth, capable of clamping down with almost four times the force of a modern-day crocodile's bite. The back of the skull housed the powerful muscles that it used to chomp through its prey.

Sharp, spikelike teeth

AT A GLANCE

LENGTH 12.6 m (41 ft)

DIET Carnivore

LIVED 157–152 MYA

HABITAT Oceans

SPINY DISPLAY
AMARGASAURUS

Unlike most sauropods, which were generally large and long-necked, *Amargasaurus* belonged to a group of relatively small, short-necked sauropods called the dicraeosaurids. It stood out from its close cousins with its impressive double row of long, bony spines. The short neck of this South American herbivore suggests it could not get at high-growing foliage so it may have been mostly a ground-feeder.

MOST NECK SPINES

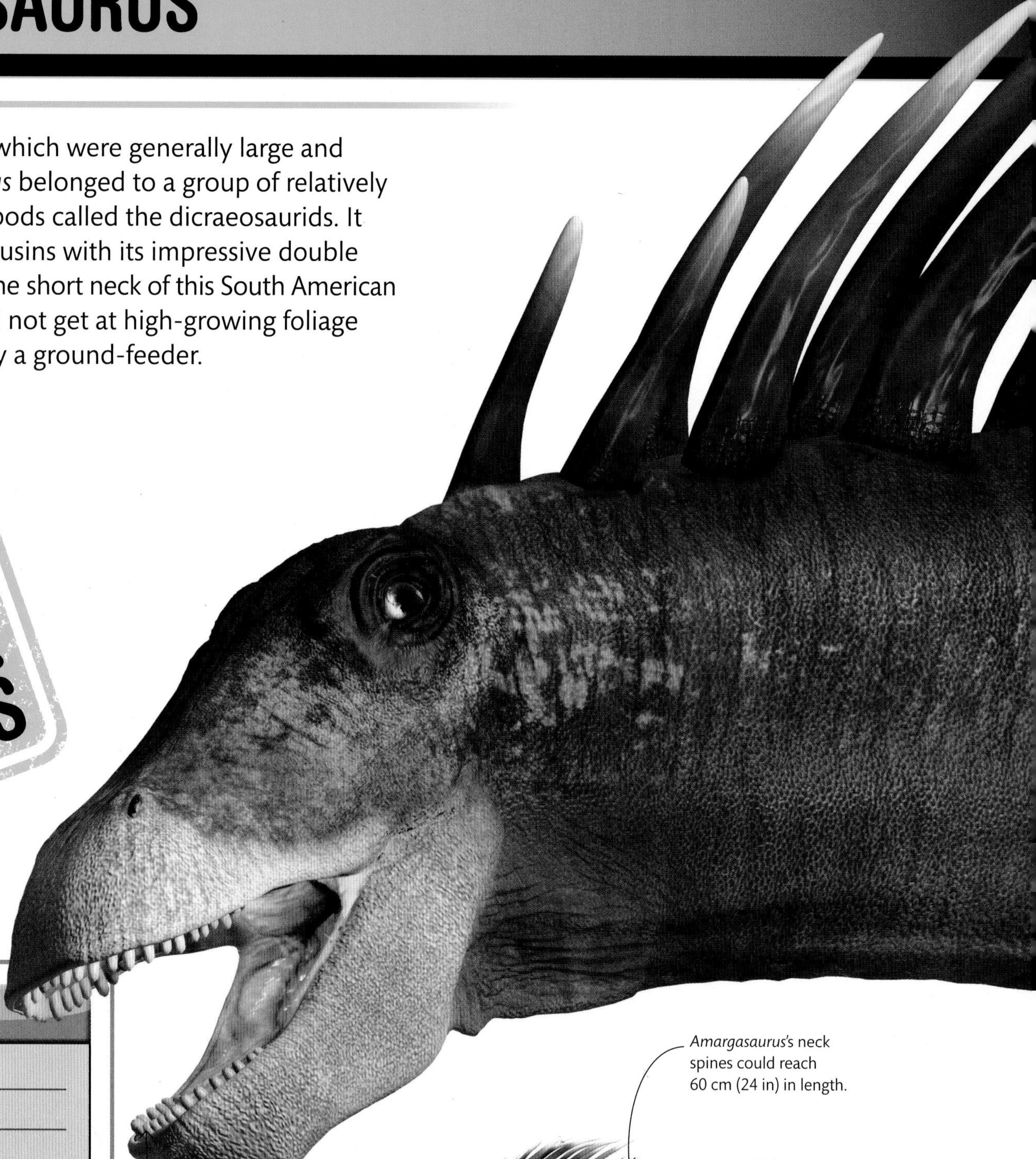

AT A GLANCE

- **LENGTH** 10 m (33 ft)
- **DIET** Herbivore
- **LIVED** 129–122 MYA
- **HABITAT** Fern prairies and open plains

Amargasaurus's neck spines could reach 60 cm (24 in) in length.

Pencil-like teeth are likely to have lined the front of *Amargasaurus*'s snout.

Extreme spines

Amargasaurus's double row of neck spines must have been visually impressive, but their exact function is not clear. Given their position high on the neck and their large size, it is possible that they were used to ward off rivals or to attract mates.

STATS AND FACTS

Amargasaurus is known to us from only one nearly complete fossil. Discovered in 1984, this fossil was found in the sedimentary rocks of the La Amarga Formation in Argentina, from which *Amargasaurus* gets its name.

DIET

Amargasaurus would eat about 9–20 kg (20–44 lb) of plants per day, which is significantly less than other sauropods.

FEEDING RANGE

Amargasaurus could only reach plants up to 2.7 m (9 ft) above the ground.

A flamingo-like diet of brine shrimp may have given *Pterodaustro* a pinkish hue.

STATS AND FACTS

The bristly structures in *Pterodaustro*'s mouth resemble the baleen plates that line the jaws of modern filter-feeding whales. However, studies of these structures tell us that they are not plates at all, but simply specialized teeth made up of the same materials as the teeth of most other animals.

TINY UPPER TEETH

Measuring just 1 mm (¹⁄₃₂ in) across, the teeth in the upper jaw were only used to crush prey.

COMMON PTEROSAUR

With 300 known fossils, this pterosaur is one of the best known from South America.

Pterodaustro's wings could fold up against its body when it was on the ground.

AT A GLANCE

- **WINGSPAN** 2.5 m (8 ft)
- **DIET** Carnivore
- **LIVED** 113–101 MYA
- **HABITAT** Lakes and coasts

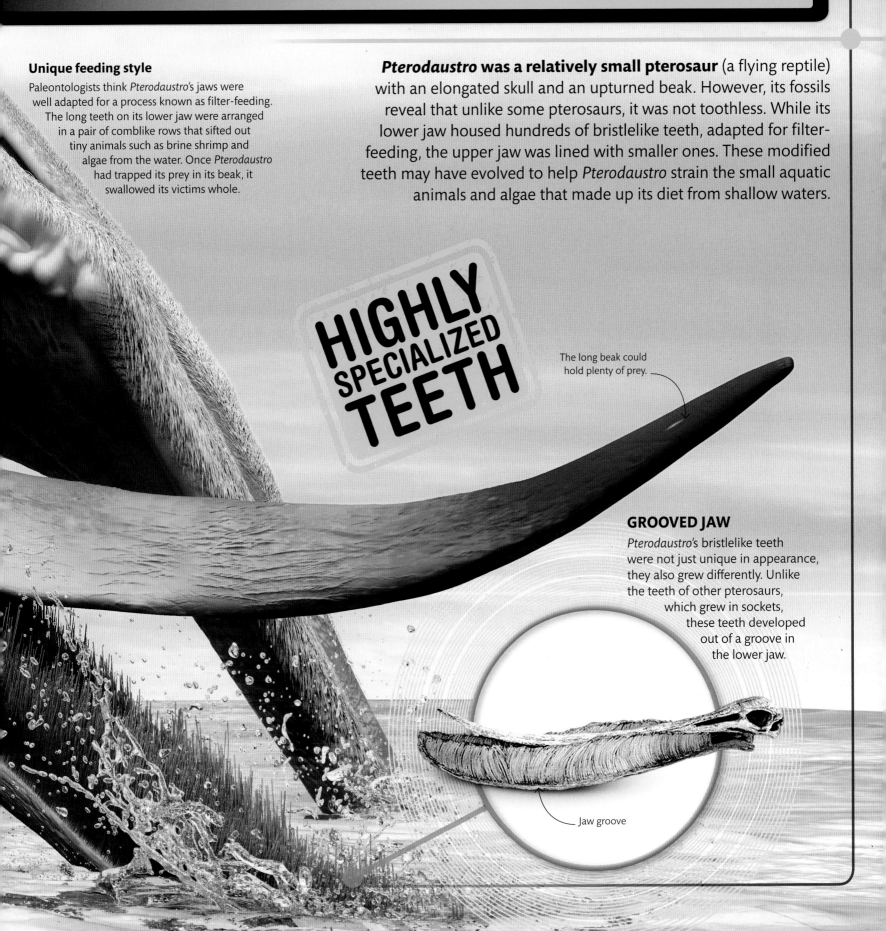

Unique feeding style

Paleontologists think *Pterodaustro*'s jaws were well adapted for a process known as filter-feeding. The long teeth on its lower jaw were arranged in a pair of comblike rows that sifted out tiny animals such as brine shrimp and algae from the water. Once *Pterodaustro* had trapped its prey in its beak, it swallowed its victims whole.

Pterodaustro **was a relatively small pterosaur** (a flying reptile) with an elongated skull and an upturned beak. However, its fossils reveal that unlike some pterosaurs, it was not toothless. While its lower jaw housed hundreds of bristlelike teeth, adapted for filter-feeding, the upper jaw was lined with smaller ones. These modified teeth may have evolved to help *Pterodaustro* strain the small aquatic animals and algae that made up its diet from shallow waters.

HIGHLY
SPECIALIZED
TEETH

The long beak could hold plenty of prey.

GROOVED JAW

Pterodaustro's bristlelike teeth were not just unique in appearance, they also grew differently. Unlike the teeth of other pterosaurs, which grew in sockets, these teeth developed out of a groove in the lower jaw.

Jaw groove

BEAK OF BRISTLES

As this fossil cast shows, the pterosaur *Pterodaustro* had long, thin, bristly teeth in its beak. Unlike modern birds, many prehistoric flying reptiles had teeth, but *Pterodaustro's* were uniquely adapted for filter feeding. *Pterodaustro* probably fed on the tiny shrimp and algae that lived in its lakeside habitat, using its sievelike beak to filter them out of the water. Like modern flamingos, *Pterodaustro* nested along the edges of the lake.

SAIL-BACKED GIANT
SPINOSAURUS

The North African giant *Spinosaurus* probably spent a lot of time in and around water, perhaps to avoid competing with other fierce carnivores on land. The creature's huge 1.7-m (5½-ft) long skull, powerfully built arms, and large claws tell us that this mighty predator could have easily caught and eaten a range of prey, including fish, and could even take down medium-sized dinosaurs. For many years there was only one known *Spinosaurus* fossil, which was destroyed during World War II. Since then, its anatomy and behaviour have become a topic of heated debate among paleontologists. Recent findings have helped shed more light on how this theropod with a spectacular "sail" on its back might have hunted and fed.

AT A GLANCE

● **LENGTH** 15 m (49 ft)

● **DIET** Carnivore

● **LIVED** 110–95 MYA

● **HABITAT** Swamps

STATS AND FACTS

The first fossil of this theropod was found by Richard Markgraf in the Bahariya Oasis in western Egypt in 1912. It was named *Spinosaurus*, meaning "spined reptile", by the German paleontologist Ernst Stromer in 1915.

WEIGHT

The few remains of *Spinosaurus* suggest that it may have weighed up to 6.5 tonnes.

SPINE HEIGHT

The spines on *Spinosaurus*'s back were nearly 2 m (6½ ft) tall.

LARGEST SAIL

Sail enigma

The exact use of the tall spines and sail projecting from *Spinosaurus*'s back bones is unclear. Scientists have suggested a range of possible purposes – from temperature control to fat storage, or even display.

Spinosaurus may have preyed on the prehistoric swordfish *Onchopristis*.

HUNTING EXPERT

Spinosaurus's skull and teeth resembled those of modern crocodiles. Like present-day reptiles, *Spinosaurus* had ridged teeth without serrations, which would have improved its grip on slippery prey such as fish.

Tyrannosaurus's forward-facing eyes helped it judge distances perfectly.

Tyrannosaurus had deadly teeth that could slice into its prey's flesh with ease.

Tiny forearms

Tyrannosaurus needed strong thigh muscles to power its huge legs.

Violent brawling

Skull biting appears to have been a common behaviour in the tyrannosaurid family, indicating they often fought, and sometimes ate, one another. Many tyrannosaur skull bones, including some from youngsters, have been found with tooth marks and gouges.

STATS AND FACTS

8.9 TONNES
WEIGHT OF AN ADULT T REX

Tyrannosaurus grew rapidly during its teenage years, packing on the pounds at a rate of around 600 kg (1,323 lb) per year – which is almost 2 kg (4½ lb) a day!

SPEED

Recent research suggests that Tyrannosaurus may not have been very fast, with a top speed of about 20–29 km/h (12–18 mph).

ARMS

Tyrannosaurus's tiny arms were strongly built, and could lift up to 200 kg (441 lb) in weight.

TERRIFYING TYRANT
TYRANNOSAURUS

Large, deadly, bipedal theropods called tyrannosaurids, which had massive skulls, sharp teeth, and powerful bodies, became the dominant carnivores in the northern hemisphere by the Late Cretaceous Period. Of all the terrifying creatures in this family, *Tyrannosaurus* was probably the biggest and most fearsome. Known from more than 50 well-preserved fossils, it is one of the best-studied and most famous dinosaurs in the world. *Tyrannosaurus's* big, bulky body, well-muscled legs, and powerful bite made it the top predator of its time, and it could even take down the most sizeable prey, such as *Edmontosaurus*.

SHARP CLAWS

Tyrannosaurus had large, sharp claws on the ends of its forearms. While paleontologists still debate the possible purpose of the tiny arms, some have suggested that *Tyrannosaurus* could have used its claws to clasp struggling prey.

AT A GLANCE

- **LENGTH** 12 m (39 ft)
- **DIET** Carnivore
- **LIVED** 67–66 MYA
- **HABITAT** Subtropical forests and coastal swamps

KILLER CLAWS
DAKOTARAPTOR

With its large "killer claw", *Dakotaraptor* stalked the Late Cretaceous plains of what is now North America. This formidable predator had large wings, which may have helped it balance itself when lifting its feet, ready to pin its prey beneath its sharp claws. Paleontologists think that *Dakotaraptor* probably competed with younger tyrannosaurids for food. Its fossils, which were first found in the Hell Creek Formation, USA, tell us that this mid-sized hunter probably came somewhere between the tiny maniraptorans and the gigantic *Tyrannosaurus* on the predator food chain.

Dakotaraptor is **named** after the US state of South Dakota, where its fossils were first found.

Dakotaraptor was probably covered in feathers, perhaps to keep it warm or for display.

STATS AND FACTS

After studying fossils of *Dakotaraptor*'s limbs, paleontologists have come to believe it was a fast runner that might have chased down small prey. However, they are unsure whether or not *Dakotaraptor* hunted in packs.

WEIGHT

An adult *Dakotaraptor* could weigh up to 374 kg (825 lb).

FEATHERS

Ten small ridges were found on one of *Dakotaraptor*'s arm bones. These ridges, called quill knobs, are where large feathers were probably attached to its tissues.

Deadly claw

Dakotaraptor had a 24-cm (9½-in) long claw on its second toe, which it probably used to grip and pin down prey. Its teeth then tore away at its victim's flesh.

Dakotaraptor kept its long claw off the ground.

Dakotaraptor had a wrist bone that allowed it to fold its long hands back against its body.

Smaller toe claws

BIGGEST KILLER CLAW

Research suggests that *Dakotaraptor* might have used its feathers to cover and protect its eggs.

WETLAND HUNTER
BARYONYX

With its long snout full of sharp teeth, the theropod *Baryonyx* almost resembled a crocodile. Its sawlike, serrated teeth may have helped this carnivore tear into the flesh of its struggling prey. Fossils of *Baryonyx* have been found with digested fish scales as well as the bones of a baby *Iguanodon* in its rib cage. This has led scientists to think that unlike most theropods, which hunted on land, *Baryonyx* may have eaten both water- and land-based prey.

AT A GLANCE

- **LENGTH** 8.5 m (28 ft)
- **DIET** Carnivore
- **LIVED** 125 MYA
- **HABITAT** Wetlands

STATS AND FACTS

The first *Baryonyx* skeleton, discovered by fossil collector William J Walker, was named *Baryonyx walkeri*. The name "*Baryonyx*" means "heavy claw", while "*walkeri*" honours the fossil's finder.

FISH-EATER

Baryonyx was the first fish-eating dinosaur to be discovered.

TEETH

Baryonyx had more teeth than most other theropods, with 64 lining the bottom jaw alone.

Baryonyx had a small crest on its head, which may have been for display.

Curved, "S"-shaped neck

Catching prey

Paleontologists are still unsure how *Baryonyx* used its huge hand claw. While some think it was used to spear fish out of rivers, others suggest that it came in handy for tearing up carcasses.

A huge 30-cm (12-in) long claw tipped the first digit of each hand.

TURNING THE TABLES

An unlucky *Teratophoneus* has been outmanoeuvred and pinned down by its own prey. While the frilled herbivore *Utahceratops* might have made a good target for a hungry theropod like *Teratophoneus*, hunting such large prey is risky and this time the predator has come unstuck. *Teratophoneus* would be wise to go after smaller prey next time, if it can survive the battle.

TREMENDOUS TALONS

THERIZINOSAURUS

Therizinosaurus confused paleontologists for a long time. When the bones of this plant-eating theropod were first discovered, they were thought to belong to a giant turtle. It was only after fossils of similar creatures were discovered that paleontologists pieced together the biology of this remarkable animal. *Therizinosaurus* was a tall dinosaur with massive claws on each arm and a sharp beak that it used to snap up plant matter. It is currently known as the largest of the maniraptorans, a group of feathered theropods that includes creatures such as *Velociraptor* and *Oviraptor*.

Paleontologists think that *Therizinosaurus* was feathered because of evidence of feathers found on the fossils of its close relatives.

Therizinosaurus had three curved claws, which it may have used as defensive weapons to deter predators.

AT A GLANCE

LENGTH 8–11 m (26–36 ft)

DIET Herbivore

LIVED 72–66 MYA

HABITAT Forests

STATS AND FACTS

Therizinosaurus possessed the longest claws of any known modern or extinct animal. The claws were slightly curved, quite thin, and may have helped the theropod hook and pull branches down to its mouth.

CLAW LENGTH

60 cm
(24 in)

UNIQUE FOOTPRINTS

Unlike most theropods, *Therizinosaurus* left behind four-toed footprints, which are distinctive and easily identifiable.

SLOW MOVING

Although strong, this dinosaur's short legs were not built for speed, and it probably could not outrun predators.

LONGEST CLAWS

Towering plant-eater

Moving around on its hind legs, *Therizinosaurus* used its long neck to reach leaves high up on tall trees and shrubs. It shared a habitat with the giant carnivore *Tarbosaurus*, but its huge frame and giant claws probably helped keep this predator at bay.

Therizinosaurus's bulky body contained a big digestive system to help process tough vegetation.

STRONGEST BITE: LAND ANIMAL

STATS AND FACTS

Tyrannosaurus had fused nose bones that strengthened its snout. This allowed it to chomp down on its prey with incredible power, but without damaging its own skull.

SKULL LENGTH

Measuring around 1.5 m (5 ft), *Tyrannosaurus* had one of the largest skulls of all the theropods.

BITE FORCE

A *Tyrannosaurus* could generate 3.6 tonnes of bite force, while humans can only manage around 77 kg (170 lb).

AT A GLANCE

LENGTH 12 m (39 ft)

DIET Carnivore

LIVED 67–66 MYA

HABITAT Subtropical forests and coastal floodplains

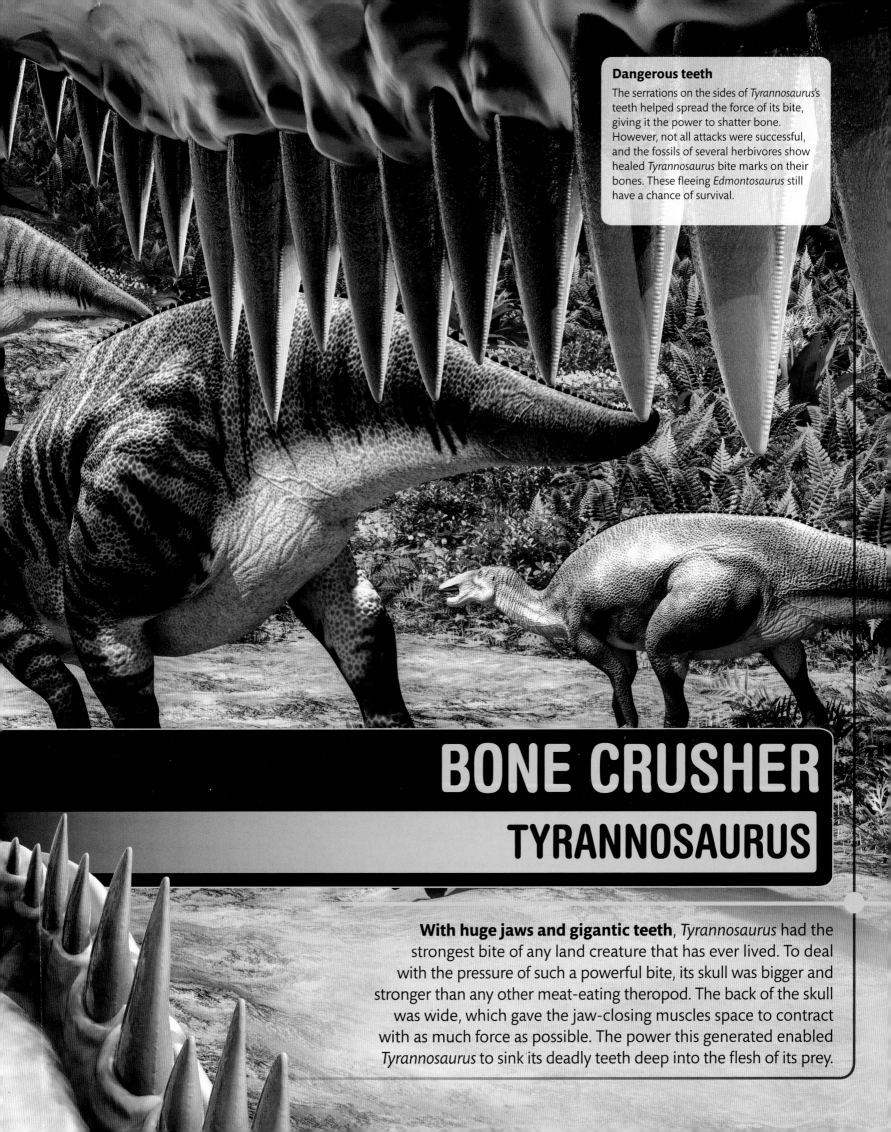

BONE CRUSHER
TYRANNOSAURUS

With huge jaws and gigantic teeth, *Tyrannosaurus* had the strongest bite of any land creature that has ever lived. To deal with the pressure of such a powerful bite, its skull was bigger and stronger than any other meat-eating theropod. The back of the skull was wide, which gave the jaw-closing muscles space to contract with as much force as possible. The power this generated enabled *Tyrannosaurus* to sink its deadly teeth deep into the flesh of its prey.

AT A GLANCE

- **LENGTH** 6 m (20 ft)
- **DIET** Carnivore
- **LIVED** 70.6–66 MYA
- **HABITAT** Polar regions

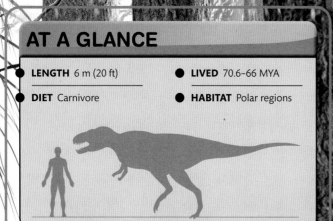

STATS AND FACTS

The word *"nanuq"* means "polar bear" in the language of the indigenous Iñupiaq people that live in northwestern Alaska, where the fossils of *Nanuqsaurus* were found. Paleontologists know very little about the appearance of this small tyrannosaurid as only three fossils have ever been found – a piece each of the upper and lower jaws, and a portion of the brain case.

TINY TEETH

Nanuqsaurus had a curious pair of teeth in the lower jaw that were less than half the size of the rest of its teeth.

SKULL SIZE

Paleontologists estimate that *Nanuqsaurus's* skull measured 60–70 cm (24–27½ in) in length.

ARCTIC TERROR
NANUQSAURUS

Some scientists suggest that *Nanuqsaurus* may have been covered in feathers that kept it warm in its freezing habitat.

One of the smallest tyrannosaurids, *Nanuqsaurus* was about half the length of its more famous cousin, *Tyrannosaurus*. Fossils of this predator were found in a rock formation called Prince Creek in what is now Alaska, USA. During the Late Cretaceous Period, tall mountains formed around this region, cutting it off from areas to the south, and stopping the animals that lived here from moving to warmer climates in search of food. The cold and dark winters in the region meant fewer plants and fewer herbivores, reducing the food supply for carnivores that preyed on them. However, *Nanuqsaurus* was able to thrive in the region because its reduced size meant that it could survive on small quantities of food.

Nanuqsaurus's skull shows that the area of its brain that dealt with smell was large, which means that it probably depended on that sense for hunting.

***Nanuqsaurus* was discovered by accident at the dig site for another dinosaur.**

Polar predator

Stalking through the icy forests of the far north, *Nanuqsaurus* faced a struggle to survive. These hunters probably fed on the young of large herbivores in its habitat such as the horned *Pachyrhinosaurus* and a hadrosaur called *Ugrunaaluk*. The slim pickings wouldn't have provided much energy, which may have limited *Nanuqsaurus*'s size and prevented it from growing as large as its cousins in the south.

AGE OF THE DINOSAURS

77

LIGHTWEIGHT RACERS
ORNITHOMIMUS

The ostrichlike *Ornithomimus* belonged to a group of long-limbed theropods called ornithomimids who shared one crucial trait: speed. With their long legs powered by strong muscles and lean, lightweight bodies, ornithomimids were probably the fastest dinosaurs to race across the face of Earth. Paleontologists have found fossils of many ornithomimids preserved together, which suggests that these swift theropods may have moved around in small groups, perhaps as a way to help keep an eye out for predators.

The tail helped these theropods balance their weight while running.

FASTEST DINOSAURS

Like all dinosaurs, *Ornithomimus* walked on its toes.

STATS AND FACTS

Ornithomimus had a toothless beak, which tells us that it was probably a herbivore but may have also eaten some small animals and insects. Fossils of some ornithomimids suggest that they swallowed stones to help break down tough plant matter in their stomach.

WEIGHT

Ornithomimus weighed about 170 kg (375 lb), while the largest ornithomimid, *Gallimimus*, weighed 440 kg (970 lb).

HOLLOW BONES

Ornithomimids had hollow bones, much like modern-day birds, which made them very light.

RUNNING SPEED

60 KM/H (37 MPH)

A birdlike, toothless beak helped *Ornithomimus* crop vegetation with ease.

Built for speed

Fossils of ornithomimid skeletons show several characteristics that suggest these creatures were fast runners. Like modern ostriches, the long limbs of these dinosaurs gave them a lengthy stride. The bones of their feet were strongly built to absorb the impact of running at speed.

Most of *Ornithomimus's* body was covered in fine, fuzz-like feathers.

AT A GLANCE

- **LENGTH** 3–4 m (10–13 ft)
- **DIET** Herbivore
- **LIVED** 72–66 MYA
- **HABITAT** Open plains and riverbanks

RUNNING FOR COVER

This trio of *Thescelosaurus* scramble across a Late Cretaceous forest in what is now North America, perhaps in a bid to escape a predator. A 3-m (10-ft) long ornithopod, *Thescelosaurus* was one of the final dinosaurs to evolve before the end of the Mesozoic Era. It likely spent its days browsing through low-lying vegetation.

FASTEST LARGE THEROPOD

Speeding through

Research suggests that *Carnotaurus's* tail bones anchored large leg-pulling muscles, which may have propelled the creature to high speeds. The top speed of this theropod is believed to have been about 56 km/h (35 mph) – about the same as that of a leopard.

MEGA RACER
CARNOTAURUS

This formidable abelisaurid (a type of large theropod) stalked the woodlands and forests of Late Cretaceous South America. *Carnotaurus* is known from the fossils of one very well-preserved skeleton that includes an almost intact skull. This skull, which had a pair of unusual brow-horns and was lined with small, serrated teeth, was probably the creature's main weapon. *Carnotaurus* had small arms that were of limited use and lacked a moveable elbow or wrist bones. Its long tail and hefty hind legs were equipped with strong muscles that enabled it to run swiftly, making it the fastest large theropod of its time.

SKULL POWER

Carnotaurus's skull was relatively short compared to that of most other large carnivores. This theropod had two 15-cm (6-in) long horns, which might have been used in shoving matches, perhaps to fight for territory or mates.

A fossilized skin sample shows that *Carnotaurus* had tiny, pebble-like scales on its body.

AT A GLANCE

- **LENGTH** 7.8 m (25½ ft)
- **DIET** Carnivore
- **LIVED** 72–70 MYA
- **HABITAT** Woodlands and forests

HEFTY HERBIVORE
SHANTUNGOSAURUS

The heavyweight *Shantungosaurus* is the largest of a group of plant-eating dinosaurs called the ornithopods. *Shantungosaurus* had a broad beaklike mouth and strong jaws lined with hundreds of teeth that allowed this herbivore to turn even the toughest plant matter into the mushy pulp that fuelled its bulky body. Herds of these massive plant-guzzlers probably marched across the plains and swamps of Cretaceous China, making the most of the region's lush vegetation.

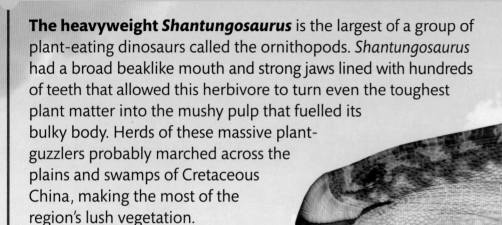

The jaws were packed with more than 1,500 chewing teeth.

STATS AND FACTS

Paleontologists have discovered fossils of more than 3,000 *Shantungosaurus* bones, belonging to 55 individuals, in a quarry in China. Undamaged by other scavenging animals, these fossils suggest that this herd may have been rapidly buried, perhaps during a devastating flash flood.

WEIGHT

The oldest *Shantungosaurus* adults may have weighed up to 16 tonnes, but only a few grew so large.

LENGTH OF THIGH BONE

The longest bone in a *Shantungosaurus* skeleton is the huge thigh bone, which measures up to 1.7 m (5½ ft).

Strength in numbers

Shantungosaurus probably moved in herds, which provided some safety from the deadly predators of the region. The sight of a herd of these giants marching together would have made hunters, such as the terrifying *Zhuchengtyrannus* (a large tyrannosaurid), think twice about an attack.

AT A GLANCE

- **LENGTH** 15 m (49 ft)
- **DIET** Herbivore
- **LIVED** 78–74 MYA
- **HABITAT** Open plains

Strong leg muscles helped support *Shantungosaurus*'s weight.

LARGEST ORNITHOPOD

Attention grabber

Ouranosaurus's sail was made of bones that grew out of its spine. Recent research has shown that younger individuals had small sails that grew to full size as the creature aged. This has led paleontologists to believe that the sail was probably used for display, helping larger, older individuals to attract mates.

Clawed forelimb

SUPER SAIL
OURANOSAURUS

This Early Cretaceous giant spent a lot of time browsing on vegetation near rivers in what is now Niger in West Africa. *Ouranosaurus*'s hooflike middle fingers and strong wrist bones suggest that it walked on all fours, but it may have reared up on its hind limbs to reach food, or to pick up speed. When its fossils were first studied in 1976, paleontologists couldn't agree on the function of *Ouranosaurus*'s large back sail. Suggested uses range from the control of body temperature to the storage of fat. Scientists are still unsure of its function today.

Large, humplike sail

LARGEST **SAIL:** ORNITHOPODS

Beaklike mouth

AT A GLANCE

- **LENGTH** 6–8 m (20–26 ft)
- **DIET** Herbivore
- **LIVED** 125–112 MYA
- **HABITAT** Arid floodplains

STATS AND FACTS

Only tough, heat-tolerant plants grew in *Ouranosaurus*'s arid home in what is now West Africa. The giant herbivore's wide beak, which had large serrated teeth, could make the most of this rough foliage.

THUMB SPIKE

Ouranosaurus had a small thumb spike, which it may have used for defence or for foraging.

SPINE HEIGHT

The tallest spines in *Ouranosaurus*'s back sail could reach a height of 64 cm (25 in).

Edmontosaurus's large, downturned bill was useful for cropping large chunks of vegetation.

Eyes on the side of Edmontosaurus's head helped it scan for lurking predators.

AT A GLANCE

- **LENGTH** 13 m (43 ft)
- **DIET** Herbivore
- **LIVED** 73–66 MYA
- **HABITAT** Forests and swamps

PLANT PROCESSOR
EDMONTOSAURUS

One of the last species to evolve from a long line of plant-eating dinosaurs called hadrosaurs, *Edmontosaurus* first appeared in what is now North America in the Late Cretaceous Period, just before the extinction of the dinosaurs. It had almost 1,000 teeth arranged in stacks along its jaws. These stacks – called dental batteries – were the most complex set of teeth ever to have evolved, and helped *Edmontosaurus* grind down and swallow even the toughest of foods, including twigs and pine needles. Fossils suggest that unlike most other dinosaurs, *Edmontosaurus* did not shed its teeth, and used parts of the roots of older teeth as a grinding surface.

Fleshy display

A specimen belonging to one species of *Edmontosaurus* was found preserved with a small, fleshy crest on top of its head, similar to the modern-day cockerel's comb. Paleontologists think the crest may have been used as a display feature to attract mates.

STATS AND FACTS

Edmontosaurus lived in regions that would have experienced cold and dark winters. This led some researchers to suggest a few *Edmontosaurus* herds may have migrated south to escape the chill. However, recent studies have shown that they probably stayed put and faced the cold.

REARING UP

Edmontosaurus could rear up on its hind legs and stand at around 4 m (13 ft) tall, in order to reach taller plants.

RUNNING SPEED

Paleontologists think that a young *Edmontosaurus* could reach speeds of 57 km/h (35 mph).

Some *Edmontosaurus* fossils that still have large areas of skin intact show that the hadrosaur had small scales.

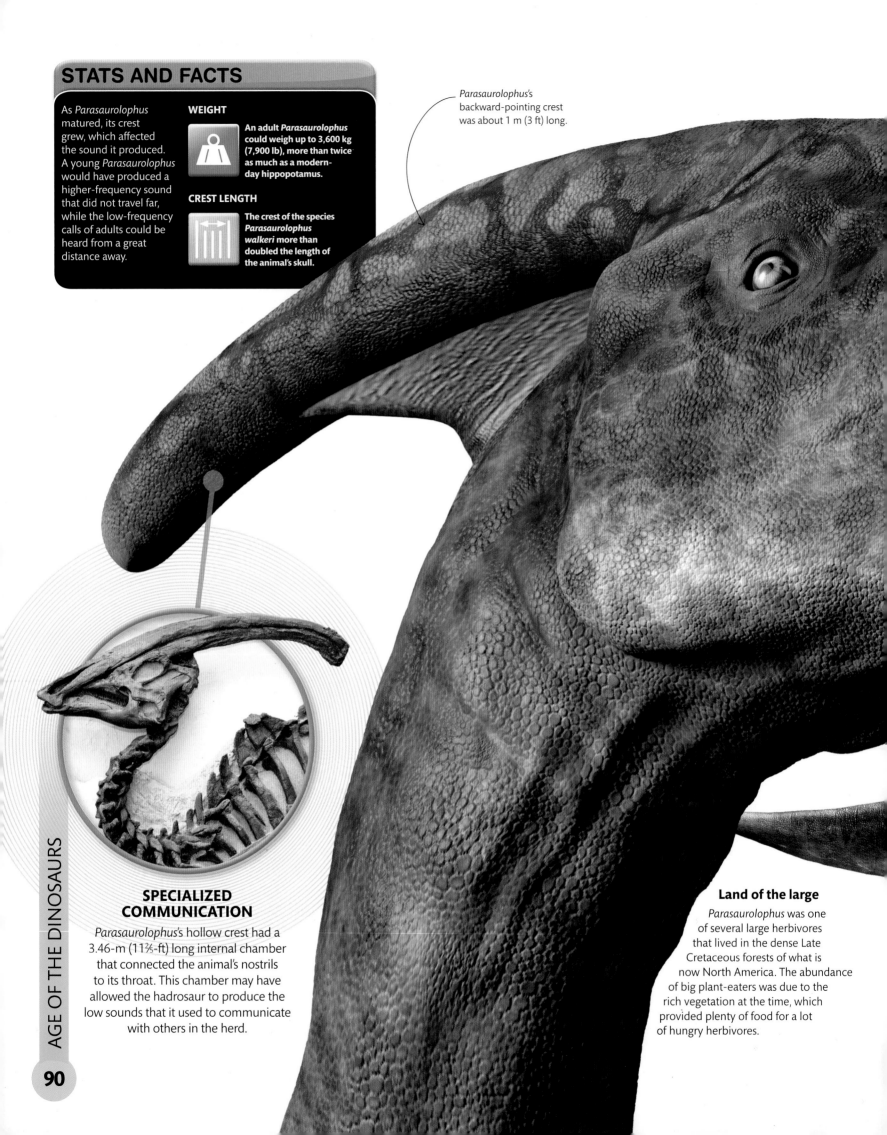

STATS AND FACTS

As *Parasaurolophus* matured, its crest grew, which affected the sound it produced. A young *Parasaurolophus* would have produced a higher-frequency sound that did not travel far, while the low-frequency calls of adults could be heard from a great distance away.

WEIGHT

An adult *Parasaurolophus* could weigh up to 3,600 kg (7,900 lb), more than twice as much as a modern-day hippopotamus.

CREST LENGTH

The crest of the species *Parasaurolophus walkeri* more than doubled the length of the animal's skull.

Parasaurolophus's backward-pointing crest was about 1 m (3 ft) long.

SPECIALIZED COMMUNICATION

Parasaurolophus's hollow crest had a 3.46-m (11⅓-ft) long internal chamber that connected the animal's nostrils to its throat. This chamber may have allowed the hadrosaur to produce the low sounds that it used to communicate with others in the herd.

Land of the large

Parasaurolophus was one of several large herbivores that lived in the dense Late Cretaceous forests of what is now North America. The abundance of big plant-eaters was due to the rich vegetation at the time, which provided plenty of food for a lot of hungry herbivores.

TUBE-CRESTED MUNCHER
PARASAUROLOPHUS

With its extravagant crest and beak, this herbivore belongs to a family of plant-eating dinosaurs called hadrosaurs. Paleontologists think that *Parasaurolophus*'s unusual tubelike crest, made of lightweight snout bones, may have helped amplify its call. A narrow beak meant *Parasaurolophus* was probably a picky eater, capable of rearing up on its hind legs to pick vegetation off taller trees. Like other hadrosaurs, it may have been able to walk on its hind limbs. It's possible *Parasaurolophus* used this ability to make itself look bigger when under threat from smaller predators.

The hadrosaur's toothless beak helped it crop vegetation with ease.

Parasaurolophus used its cheek muscles to keep food in its mouth while it chewed.

LONGEST CREST

AT A GLANCE

● **LENGTH** 9.5 m (31 ft)

● **DIET** Herbivore

● **LIVED** 76.5–73 MYA

● **HABITAT** Dense forests

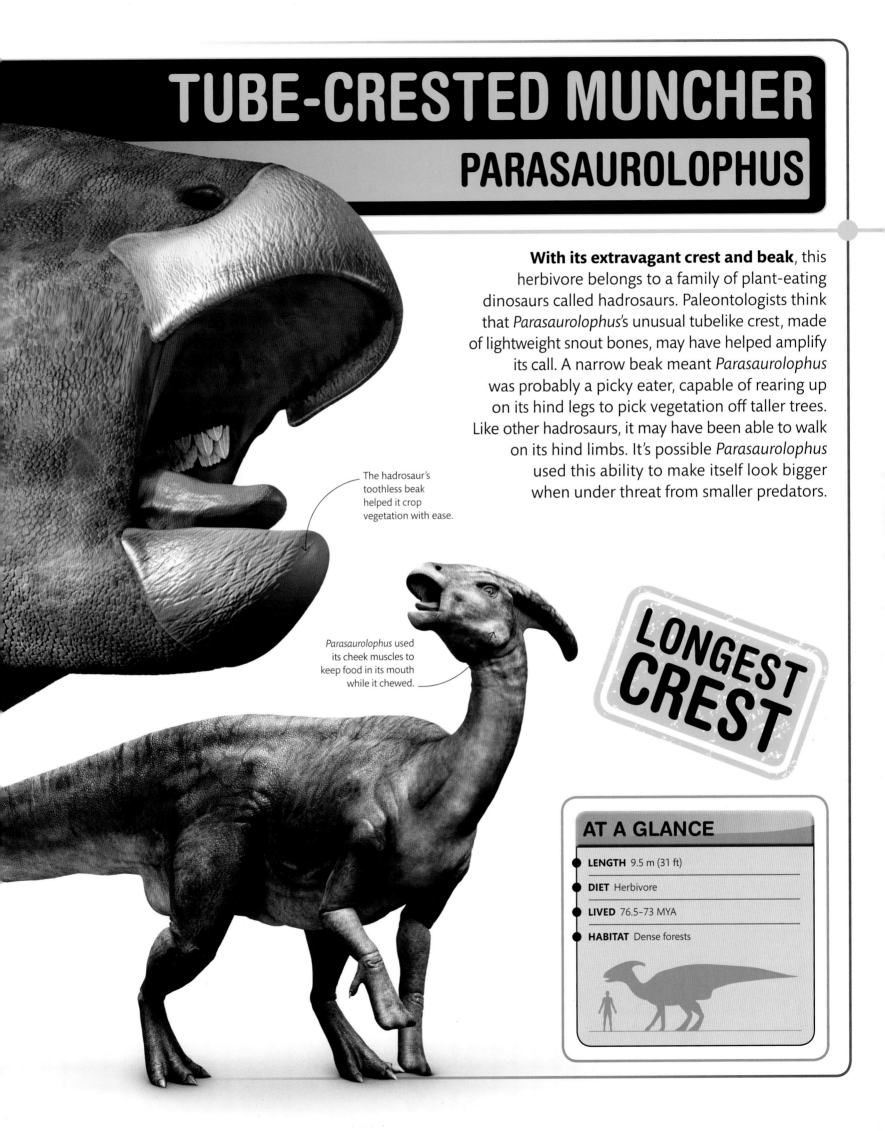

CRESTED GLIDER
PTERANODON

The giant, long-crested *Pteranodon* is one of the most spectacular flying reptiles that ever lived. It is known from hundreds of fossils, including some nearly complete skeletons, making *Pteranodon* one of the best-known pterosaurs. The flashy crest on this pterosaur's head, which may have differed in size between males and females, is perhaps its most distinctive feature. It lived near the Western Interior Seaway – an inland sea that divided North America in two during the Cretaceous Period – feeding on fish and other small sea creatures. Like some present-day seabirds, *Pteranodon* would scan the waters for prey while swimming on the surface, before diving underwater to catch its unsuspecting victim with its long, toothless beak.

At the edge of each wing, *Pteranodon* had three clawed fingers, which probably helped it walk on the ground.

AT A GLANCE

- **WINGSPAN** 6–7 m (20–23 ft)
- **DIET** Fish eater
- **LIVED** 84–71 MYA
- **HABITAT** Oceans

STATS AND FACTS

Like the lungs of modern birds, pterosaur lungs contained air sacs – little growths of tissue that push air into the lungs. These air sacs and the hollow bones of these creatures gave them lightweight bodies, letting the pterosaurs take to the air easily.

WEIGHT

Pteranodon weighed only around 20–40 kg (44–88 lb) due to its hollow bones.

FOSSILS

About 1,100 fossils of *Pteranodon* have been discovered so far.

Air and land

Pteranodon's kite-shaped body and huge wingspan helped it glide through the air with ease. When on the ground, it probably walked on all fours, folding its wings to its sides.

The crests of *Pteranodon* males could reach up to 60 cm (23½ in) in length.

LARGE CREST

Pteranodon males had a large crest on their head that they may have used to attract mates. Females probably had a much smaller crest.

Female

Male

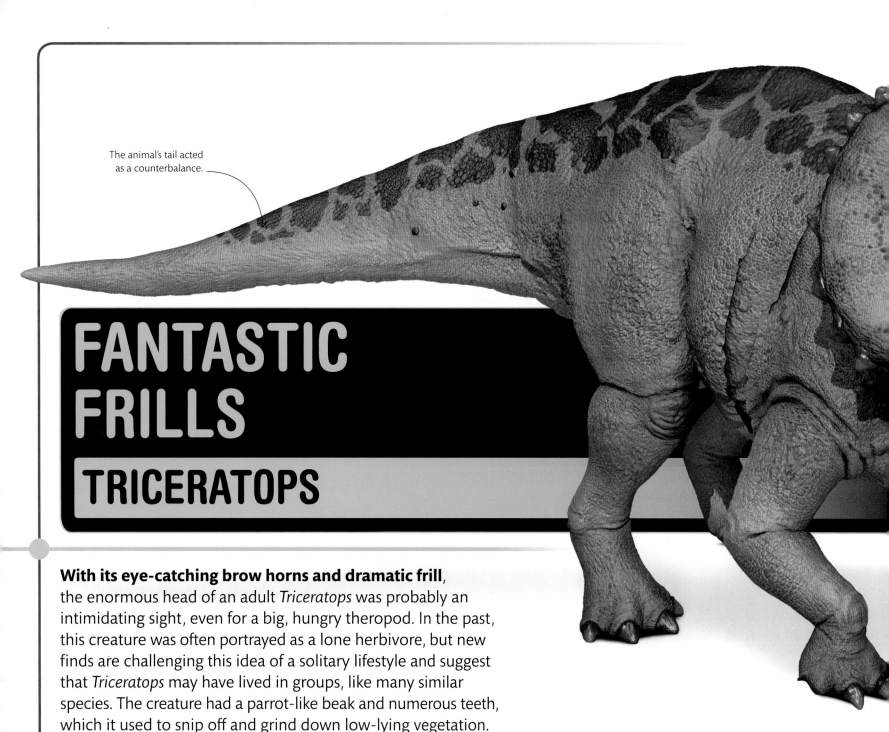

The animal's tail acted as a counterbalance.

FANTASTIC FRILLS
TRICERATOPS

With its eye-catching brow horns and dramatic frill, the enormous head of an adult *Triceratops* was probably an intimidating sight, even for a big, hungry theropod. In the past, this creature was often portrayed as a lone herbivore, but new finds are challenging this idea of a solitary lifestyle and suggest that *Triceratops* may have lived in groups, like many similar species. The creature had a parrot-like beak and numerous teeth, which it used to snip off and grind down low-lying vegetation.

AT A GLANCE

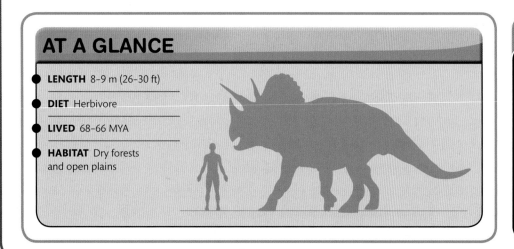

- **LENGTH** 8–9 m (26–30 ft)
- **DIET** Herbivore
- **LIVED** 68–66 MYA
- **HABITAT** Dry forests and open plains

STATS AND FACTS

Triceratops was one of the last non-bird dinosaurs to evolve in the Cretaceous Period. Its skulls are common in the Late Cretaceous rocks of North America, most likely due to their bulky size, which helped them withstand the test of time.

HORN SIZE

Triceratops had two brow horns, which grew to 1.3 m (4 ft), and had strong bony cores.

WEIGHT

Paleontologists estimate that the weight of this huge herbivore could have ranged from 5 to 14 tonnes.

Triceratops's neck frill was made of solid bone.

Triceratops's horns were covered in a tough outer casing.

CHANGING SHAPE

Skull fossils of _Triceratops_ show that the frill and horns changed shape and size as the animal aged. This has helped paleontologists understand how this dinosaur's appearance developed as it grew up.

POWERFUL HORNS

Triceratops's sturdy limbs supported its heavy frame.

Fight club

Compared to the fossils of similar animals, the skull fossils of _Triceratops_ contain a lot more injuries. The injuries suggest that these hulking herbivores may have locked horns with each other, gouging the bones of the frill and snout. These encounters were probably never fatal and some injuries show signs of healing.

FRILLED FEEDER

This pair of *Kosmoceratops* probably spent the majority of their time resting and eating huge quantities of plant matter. While these giant herbivores look well armed with bony frills and horns, it is likely that they only had to use these defences rarely. Like other ceratopsians, they may have used their fancy frills to attract mates.

TITANIC SKULL
TITANOCERATOPS

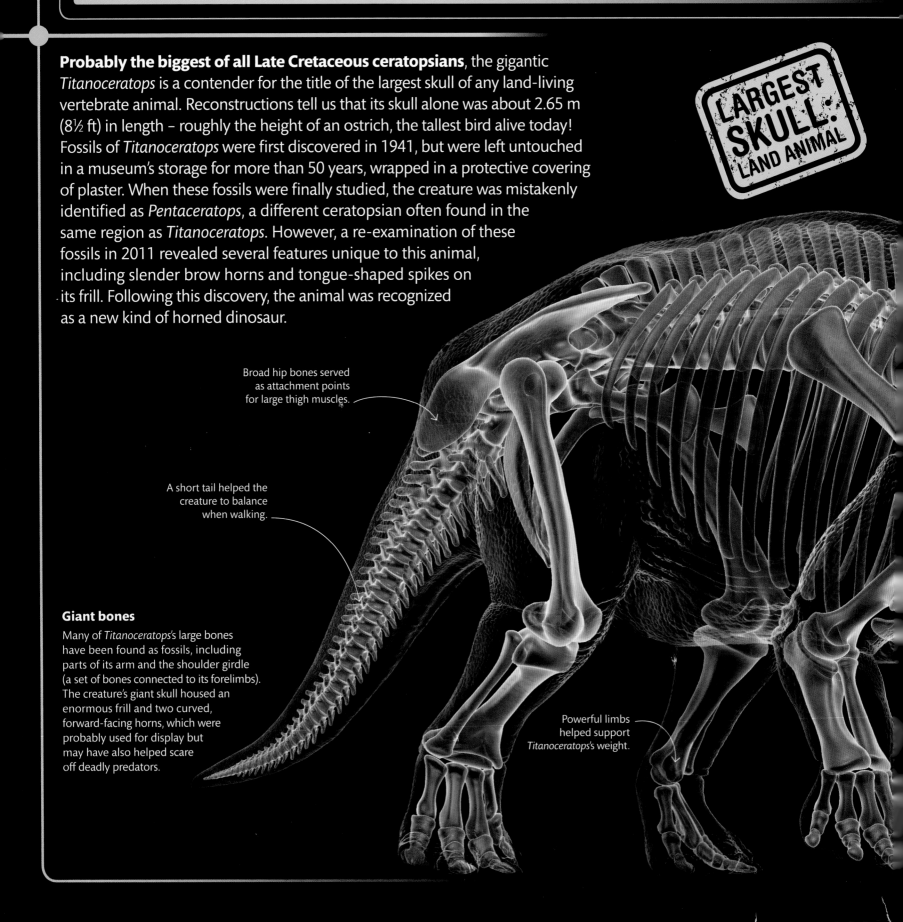

Probably the biggest of all Late Cretaceous ceratopsians, the gigantic *Titanoceratops* is a contender for the title of the largest skull of any land-living vertebrate animal. Reconstructions tell us that its skull alone was about 2.65 m (8½ ft) in length – roughly the height of an ostrich, the tallest bird alive today! Fossils of *Titanoceratops* were first discovered in 1941, but were left untouched in a museum's storage for more than 50 years, wrapped in a protective covering of plaster. When these fossils were finally studied, the creature was mistakenly identified as *Pentaceratops*, a different ceratopsian often found in the same region as *Titanoceratops*. However, a re-examination of these fossils in 2011 revealed several features unique to this animal, including slender brow horns and tongue-shaped spikes on its frill. Following this discovery, the animal was recognized as a new kind of horned dinosaur.

LARGEST SKULL: LAND ANIMAL

Broad hip bones served as attachment points for large thigh muscles.

A short tail helped the creature to balance when walking.

Giant bones

Many of *Titanoceratops*'s large bones have been found as fossils, including parts of its arm and the shoulder girdle (a set of bones connected to its forelimbs). The creature's giant skull housed an enormous frill and two curved, forward-facing horns, which were probably used for display but may have also helped scare off deadly predators.

Powerful limbs helped support *Titanoceratops*'s weight.

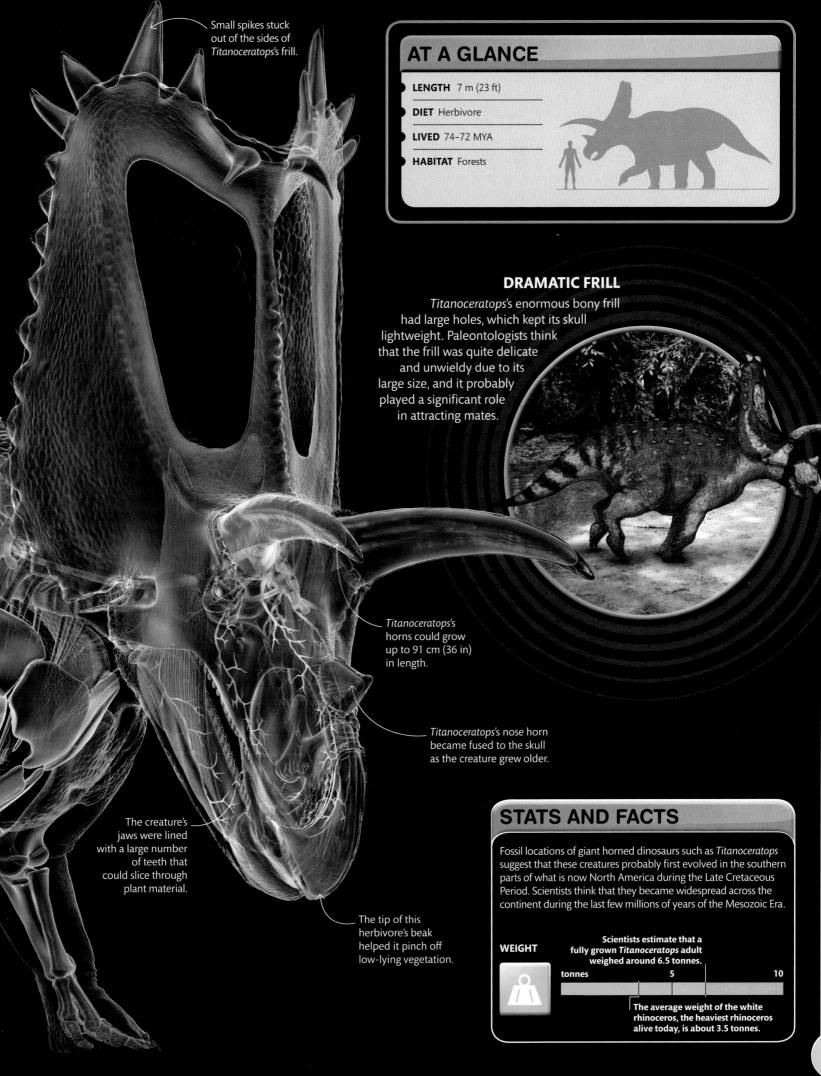

Small spikes stuck out of the sides of *Titanoceratops*'s frill.

DRAMATIC FRILL

Titanoceratops's enormous bony frill had large holes, which kept its skull lightweight. Paleontologists think that the frill was quite delicate and unwieldy due to its large size, and it probably played a significant role in attracting mates.

Titanoceratops's horns could grow up to 91 cm (36 in) in length.

Titanoceratops's nose horn became fused to the skull as the creature grew older.

The creature's jaws were lined with a large number of teeth that could slice through plant material.

The tip of this herbivore's beak helped it pinch off low-lying vegetation.

STATS AND FACTS

Fossil locations of giant horned dinosaurs such as *Titanoceratops* suggest that these creatures probably first evolved in the southern parts of what is now North America during the Late Cretaceous Period. Scientists think that they became widespread across the continent during the last few millions of years of the Mesozoic Era.

WEIGHT

Scientists estimate that a fully grown *Titanoceratops* adult weighed around 6.5 tonnes.

tonnes	5	10

The average weight of the white rhinoceros, the heaviest rhinoceros alive today, is about 3.5 tonnes.

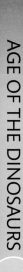

PARROT-BEAKED HERBIVORE
PSITTACOSAURUS

This small herbivore lived in the Cretaceous Period and is known from hundreds of fossils that show it had a narrow, parrot-like beak and small, sharp teeth that probably helped it slice into all kinds of vegetation. An exquisitely preserved specimen found in China shows evidence of a brown back and pale underbelly. This colour pattern – with a darker back and lighter underside – helped *Psittacosaurus* camouflage itself in the dim light of its woody habitat. By studying fossilized pigments like these, paleontologists are able to work out the colours of dinosaurs.

AT A GLANCE

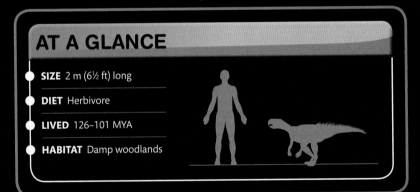

- **SIZE** 2 m (6½ ft) long
- **DIET** Herbivore
- **LIVED** 126–101 MYA
- **HABITAT** Damp woodlands

STATS AND FACTS

400
NUMBER OF FOSSILS FOUND

Using the large number of juvenile *Psittacosaurus* fossils that have been discovered, paleontologists have reconstructed this little herbivore's growth patterns. As a young *Psittacosaurus* matured, its skull shape changed, and after a few years, it began to walk upright on its hind legs.

HATCHLING SIZE

Psittacosaurus hatchlings measured 12 cm (5 in) in length and could find food for themselves without the help of adults.

WEIGHT

Psittacosaurus adults grew to 20 kg (44 lb), while youngsters have been estimated to weigh around 940 g (33 oz).

STRENGTH IN NUMBERS

Paleontologists estimate that given its large brain size, *Psittacosaurus* may have been capable of behaviour such as forming social groups or large gatherings to protect itself from predators.

STING IN THE TAIL

The tail club was made of huge osteoderms – bones that grew within the skin. To support its weight, the rear of the tail was strengthened by a framework of tough tendons and connective tissues, which helped keep the tail end rigid and clear of the ground.

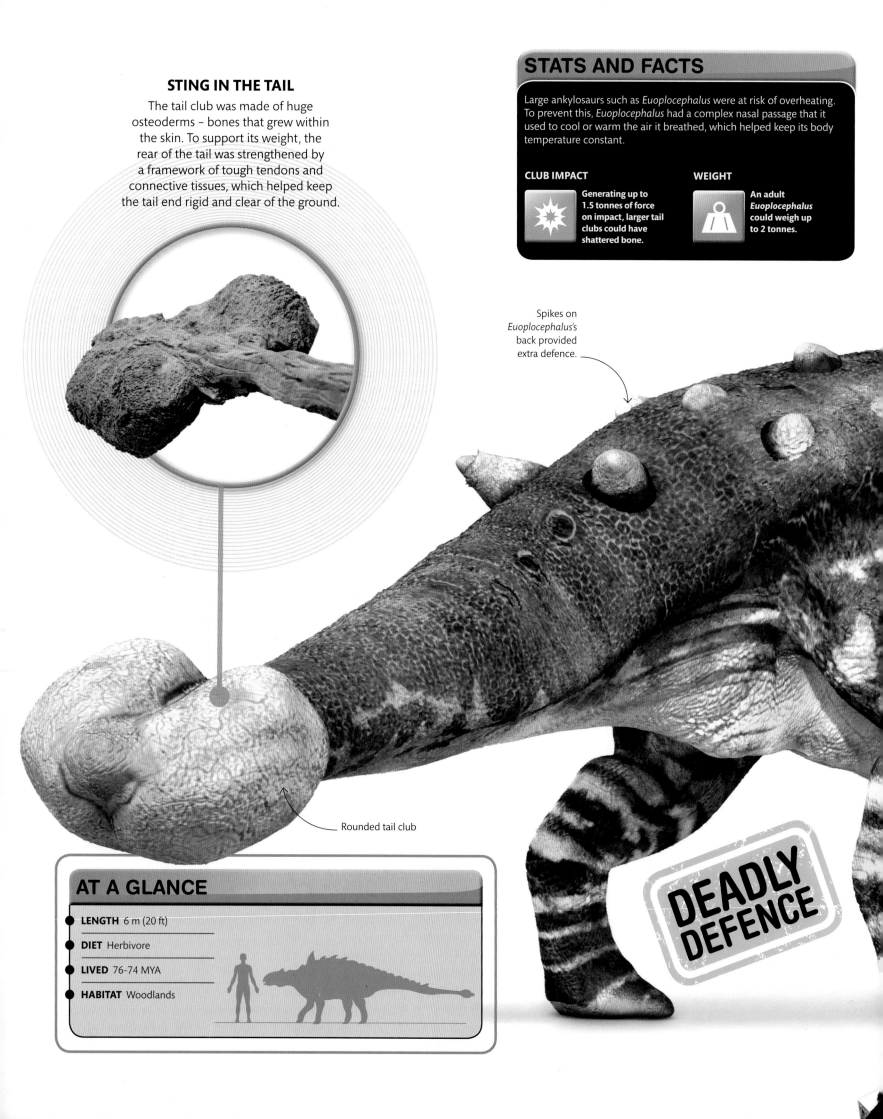

Spikes on *Euoplocephalus*'s back provided extra defence.

Rounded tail club

DEADLY DEFENCE

AT A GLANCE

- **LENGTH** 6 m (20 ft)
- **DIET** Herbivore
- **LIVED** 76-74 MYA
- **HABITAT** Woodlands

ARMOURED TANK
EUOPLOCEPHALUS

One of the best-defended dinosaurs of the Late Cretaceous Period, *Euoplocephalus* was heavily armoured and sported a wicked-looking club at the end of its tail. These defences are often thought to have evolved to help *Euoplocephalus* fend off attacks from marauding theropods but, combined with the tail club, they might have also had a role in settling disputes among its own kind. *Euoplocephalus*'s wide rib cage housed a long gut, which would have helped this hefty herbivore break down the tough, low-lying vegetation that it cropped with its broad beak. It had a wide jaw, which may have been because it wasn't a picky eater, and swallowed lots of vegetation in one mouthful.

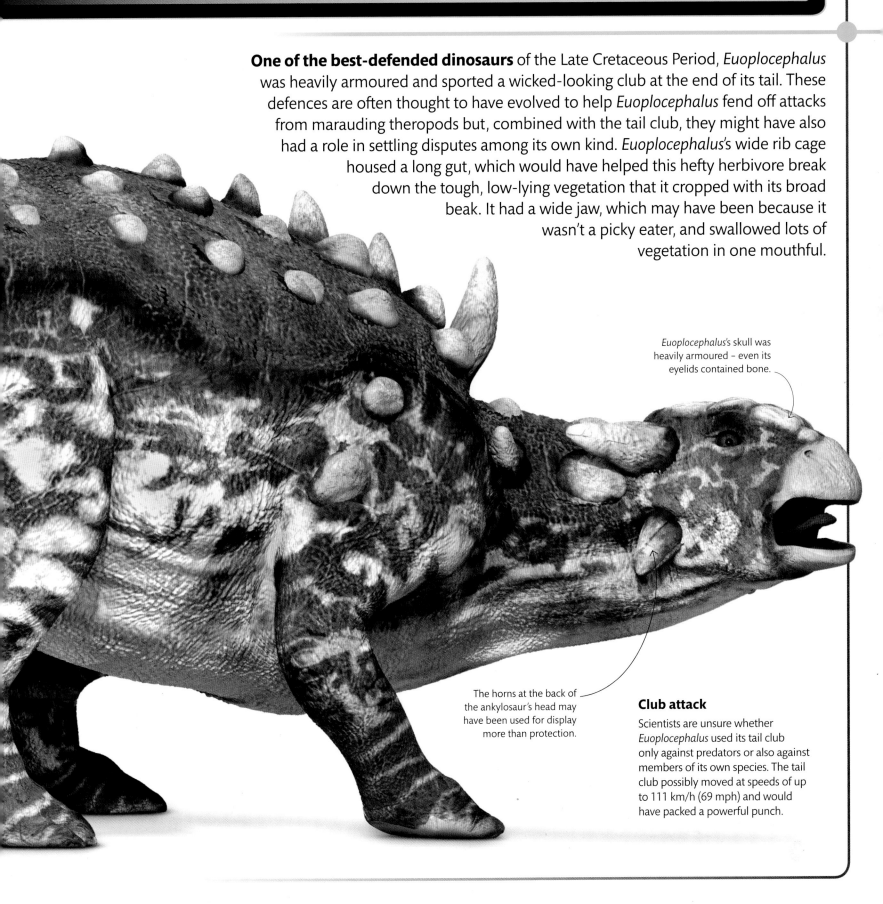

Euoplocephalus's skull was heavily armoured – even its eyelids contained bone.

The horns at the back of the ankylosaur's head may have been used for display more than protection.

Club attack

Scientists are unsure whether *Euoplocephalus* used its tail club only against predators or also against members of its own species. The tail club possibly moved at speeds of up to 111 km/h (69 mph) and would have packed a powerful punch.

HELMET HEAD
PACHYCEPHALOSAURUS

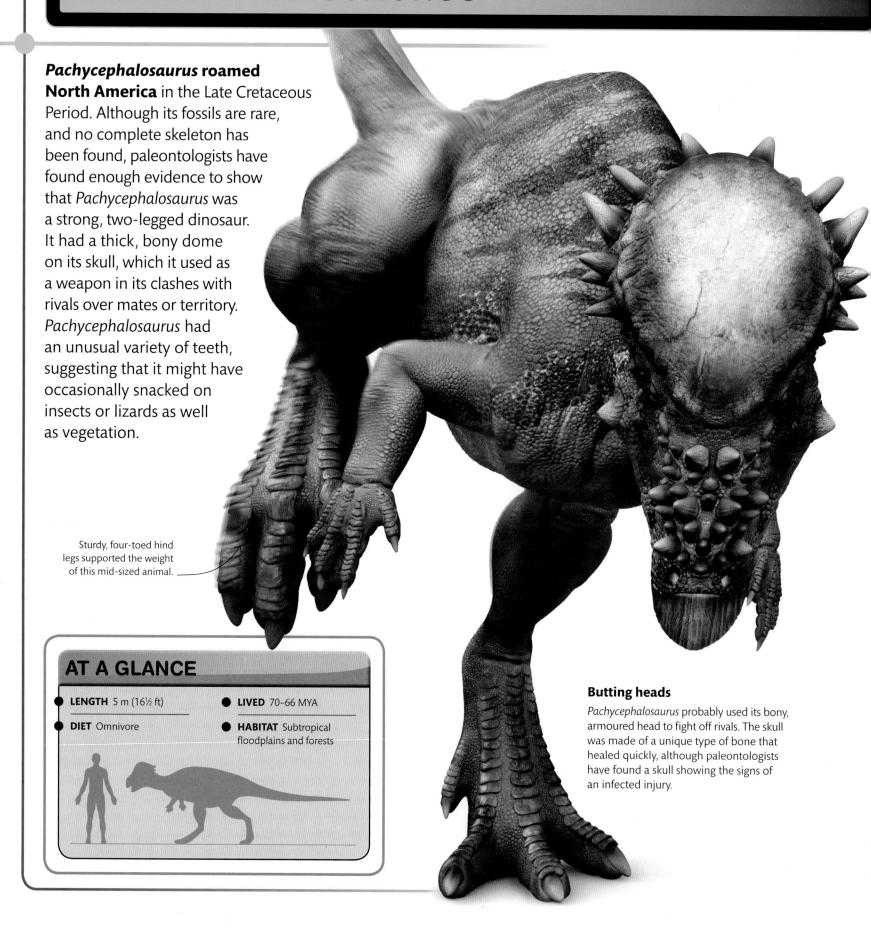

Pachycephalosaurus roamed North America in the Late Cretaceous Period. Although its fossils are rare, and no complete skeleton has been found, paleontologists have found enough evidence to show that *Pachycephalosaurus* was a strong, two-legged dinosaur. It had a thick, bony dome on its skull, which it used as a weapon in its clashes with rivals over mates or territory. *Pachycephalosaurus* had an unusual variety of teeth, suggesting that it might have occasionally snacked on insects or lizards as well as vegetation.

Sturdy, four-toed hind legs supported the weight of this mid-sized animal.

AT A GLANCE

● **LENGTH** 5 m (16½ ft)

● **LIVED** 70–66 MYA

● **DIET** Omnivore

● **HABITAT** Subtropical floodplains and forests

Butting heads

Pachycephalosaurus probably used its bony, armoured head to fight off rivals. The skull was made of a unique type of bone that healed quickly, although paleontologists have found a skull showing the signs of an infected injury.

THICKEST SKULL

The spikes around *Pachycephalosaurus*'s dome may have been for display or defence.

STATS AND FACTS

Pachycephalosaurus's skull was thicker than those of other dinosaurs. At 25 cm (10 in) thick, it was also about 40 times thicker than an average human skull.

WEIGHT

A fully grown *Pachycephalosaurus* would have weighed about 488 kg (1,076 lb).

SPEED

This dinosaur's speed at impact would have been 24 km/h (15 mph).

The hard beak helped *Pachycephalosaurus* pick off low-lying vegetation.

Pachycephalosaurus would have had scaly skin.

One fossil of a *Pachycephalosaurus* skull was found with 23 injuries.

FOOD FIGHT

Squabbles over food, like this fight for a decaying carcass, were probably quite common among theropods such as *Australovenator*, Australia's best-known predatory dinosaur. This hunter possessed large claws on its highly flexible fingers, which it may have used as a combat weapon or to grasp its prey.

A small tail fin would have helped *Albertonectes* steer through water.

Albertonectes's long flippers were made up of many digit bones.

MOST
NECK BONES

AT A GLANCE

● **LENGTH** 11–12 m (36–39 ft)

● **DIET** Fish eater

● **LIVED** 83.5–70.6 MYA

● **HABITAT** Oceans

Crunchy ammonites might have made a tasty snack for *Albertonectes*.

LONG-NECKED BEAST
ALBERTONECTES

While many of the large marine reptiles known as plesiosaurs are famous for having long necks, *Albertonectes* took this trait to the extreme. Reaching lengths of 7 m (23 ft), its elongated neck had the most bones of any known animal. *Albertonectes* was one of the last plesiosaurs to evolve before the mass extinction at the end of the Mesozoic Era. It cruised through the Western Interior Seaway – an inland sea that divided the continent of North America into two parts – during the Late Cretaceous Period. As it swam the shallow waters, it used its small head and long neck to catch fish and other marine organisms.

STATS AND FACTS

About 97 stones, some weighing up to 1 kg (2 lb), have been found among *Albertonectes*'s stomach fossils. Some of these came from beaches and riverbanks, which suggests that this creature patrolled the shorelines.

NECK BONES

Albertonectes had a record-breaking 76 bones in its neck. Its closest relatives had between 46 and 71.

SWIMMING STYLE

Albertonectes swam by moving its flippers up and down in the water like wings.

Uncertain use

Quite why some plesiosaurs evolved such immense necks is still unknown, and after more than 200 years of study paleontologists are still debating this question. Short-necked plesiosaurs would have been more flexible than *Albertonectes*, which suggests that it may have adopted a unique hunting style to accommodate its long neck.

No fossils of *Albertonectes*'s head have been found, but paleontologists think it may have looked like other plesiosaurs.

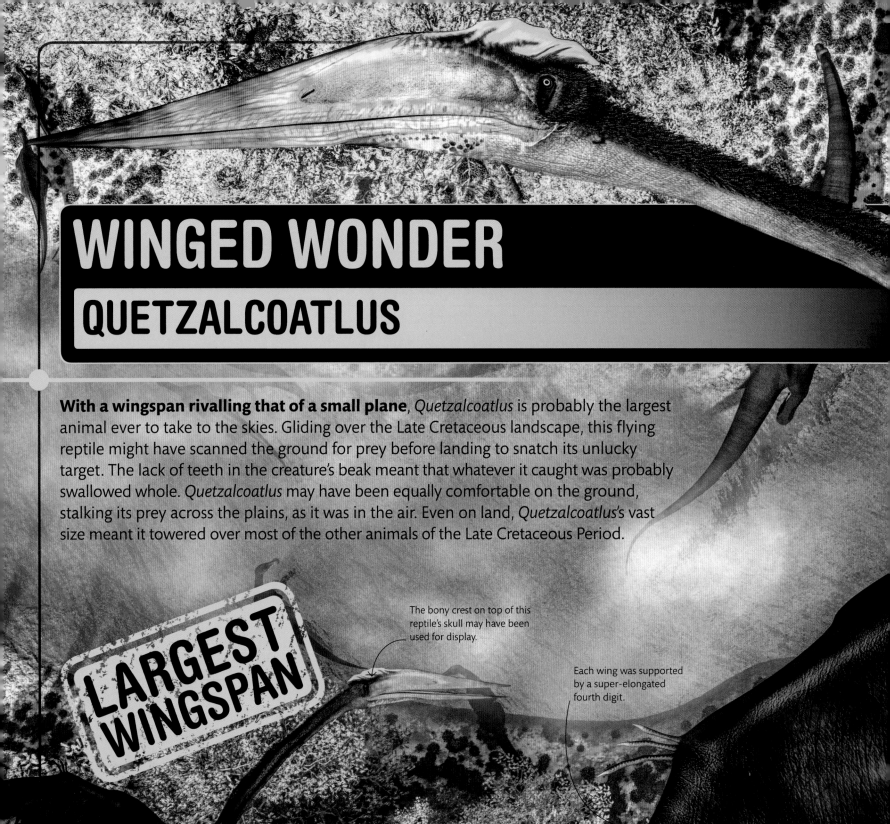

WINGED WONDER
QUETZALCOATLUS

With a wingspan rivalling that of a small plane, *Quetzalcoatlus* is probably the largest animal ever to take to the skies. Gliding over the Late Cretaceous landscape, this flying reptile might have scanned the ground for prey before landing to snatch its unlucky target. The lack of teeth in the creature's beak meant that whatever it caught was probably swallowed whole. *Quetzalcoatlus* may have been equally comfortable on the ground, stalking its prey across the plains, as it was in the air. Even on land, *Quetzalcoatlus*'s vast size meant it towered over most of the other animals of the Late Cretaceous Period.

LARGEST WINGSPAN

The bony crest on top of this reptile's skull may have been used for display.

Each wing was supported by a super-elongated fourth digit.

Quetzalcoatlus probably weighed about 240 kg (550 lb), making it fairly light for its size. In comparison, the ostrich weighs about 156 kg (344 lb) and is less than half the height of this flying reptile.

FLYING SPEED

Scientists think that *Quetzalcoatlus* could fly at speeds of about 90 km/h (56 mph).

DISTANCE

Quetzalcoatlus might have flown distances of up to 10,000 km (6,214 miles).

Giant glider

Quetzalcoatlus probably used all four of its limbs to propel itself into the air, and only flapped its wings for a short while before using air currents to glide from place to place.

Quetzalcoatlus's body was probably covered in fine hairlike structures called pycnofibres, which were made from similar materials as bird feathers.

Quetzalcoatlus was named after the **Aztec** **serpent god** **Quetzalcoatl.**

AT A GLANCE

- **WINGSPAN** 11 m (36 ft)
- **DIET** Carnivore
- **LIVED** 68–66 MYA
- **HABITAT** Continental interiors

AGE OF THE DINOSAURS

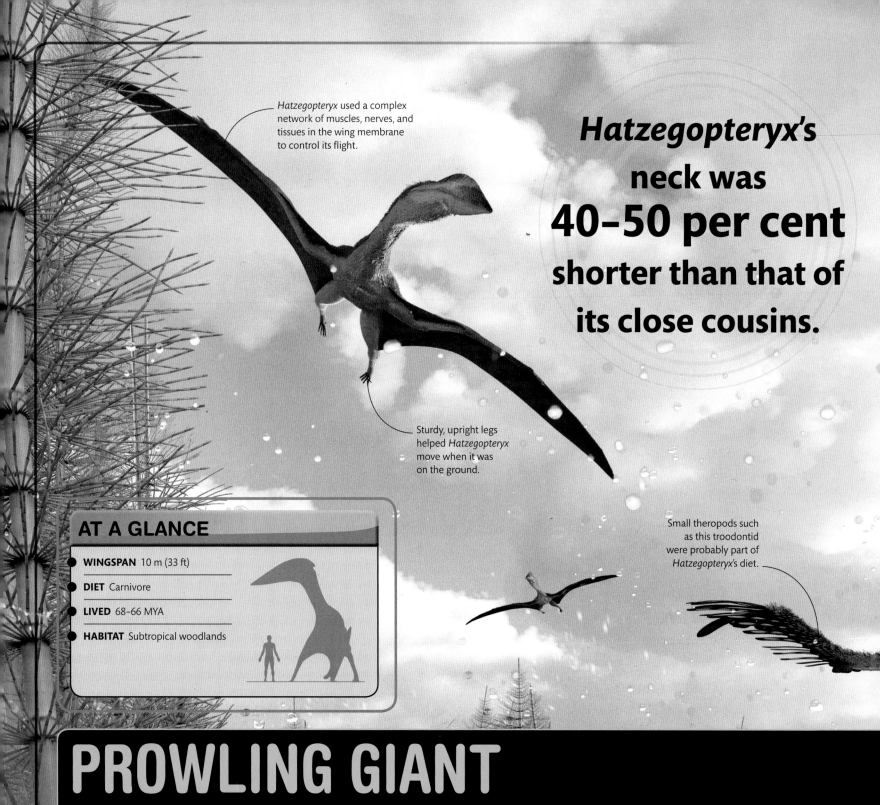

Hatzegopteryx used a complex network of muscles, nerves, and tissues in the wing membrane to control its flight.

Hatzegopteryx's neck was 40–50 per cent shorter than that of its close cousins.

Sturdy, upright legs helped *Hatzegopteryx* move when it was on the ground.

Small theropods such as this troodontid were probably part of *Hatzegopteryx's* diet.

AT A GLANCE

- **WINGSPAN** 10 m (33 ft)
- **DIET** Carnivore
- **LIVED** 68–66 MYA
- **HABITAT** Subtropical woodlands

PROWLING GIANT
HATZEGOPTERYX

With a bulkier and more muscular neck than some of its close pterosaur cousins, *Hatzegopteryx* lived on Haţeg Island, a landmass that existed millions of years ago in what is now Eastern Europe. Powered by large muscles on its arms, *Hatzegopteryx's* huge wings enabled it to cover vast distances by soaring on air currents. Its clawed feet were strong enough to support it as it tracked its prey on the ground while using its long, toothless beak to quickly snap up ground-dwelling animals, including small theropods and baby sauropods.

Island king

All known fossils of *Hatzegopteryx* have been discovered in modern-day Romania, in a region that formed an island called Haţeg during the Late Cretaceous Period. Since no evidence of other large theropods has been found there, paleontologists believe that *Hatzegopteryx* was probably the top predator on this island.

The shape of *Hatzegopteryx*'s long beak resembles those of modern ground hornbills and storks.

STATS AND FACTS

Fossils show that *Hatzegopteryx*'s skull was one of the largest of all the ground-dwelling animals discovered so far. Estimated to be 1.6–2.5 m (5–8 ft) long, its skull was about the same height as an Asian elephant.

BONE THICKNESS

Hatzegopteryx's bones were about 4–6 mm (¹⁄₁₀–⅕ in) thick.

WEIGHT

At 200–250 kg (440–550 lb), *Hatzegopteryx* was quite light for its size.

AGE OF THE DINOSAURS

113

AT A GLANCE

- **LENGTH** 80 cm (31½ in)
- **DIET** Carnivore
- **LIVED** 69–66 MYA
- **HABITAT** Forest undergrowth and floodplains

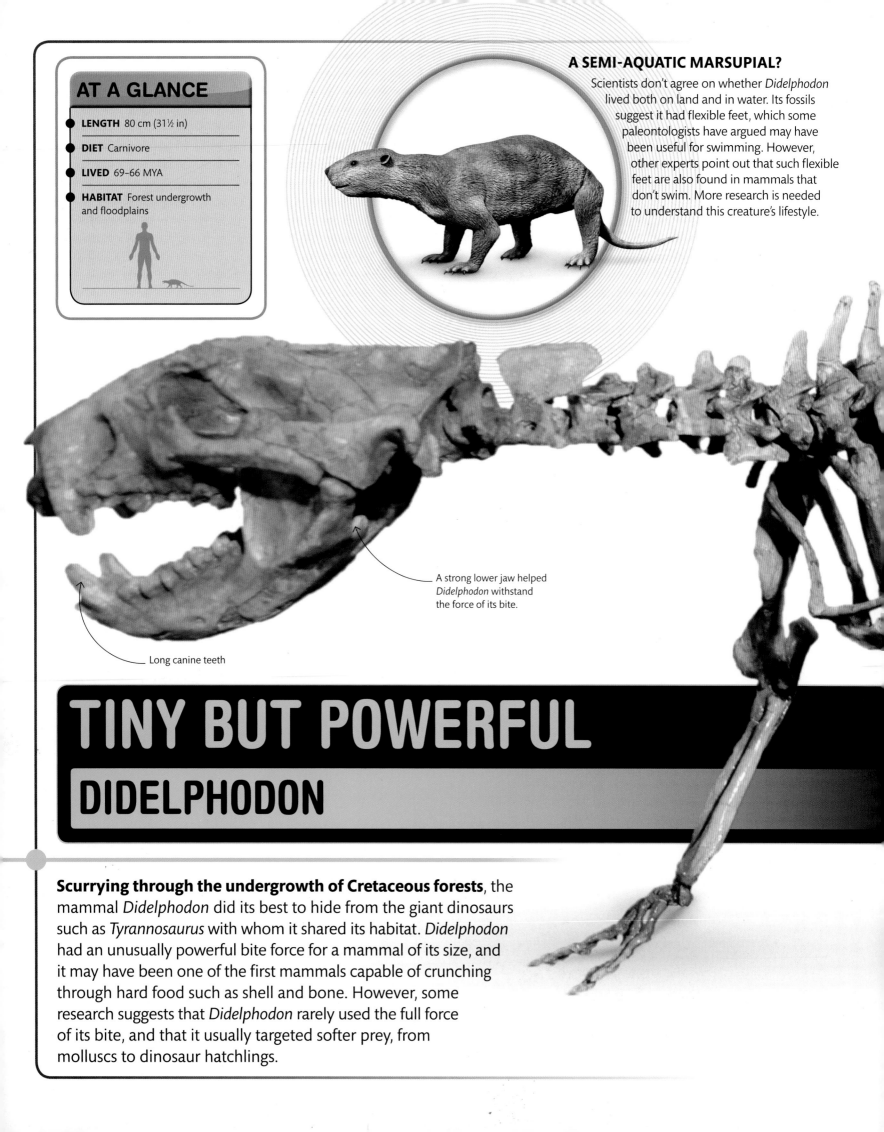

A SEMI-AQUATIC MARSUPIAL?

Scientists don't agree on whether *Didelphodon* lived both on land and in water. Its fossils suggest it had flexible feet, which some paleontologists have argued may have been useful for swimming. However, other experts point out that such flexible feet are also found in mammals that don't swim. More research is needed to understand this creature's lifestyle.

A strong lower jaw helped *Didelphodon* withstand the force of its bite.

Long canine teeth

TINY BUT POWERFUL
DIDELPHODON

Scurrying through the undergrowth of Cretaceous forests, the mammal *Didelphodon* did its best to hide from the giant dinosaurs such as *Tyrannosaurus* with whom it shared its habitat. *Didelphodon* had an unusually powerful bite force for a mammal of its size, and it may have been one of the first mammals capable of crunching through hard food such as shell and bone. However, some research suggests that *Didelphodon* rarely used the full force of its bite, and that it usually targeted softer prey, from molluscs to dinosaur hatchlings.

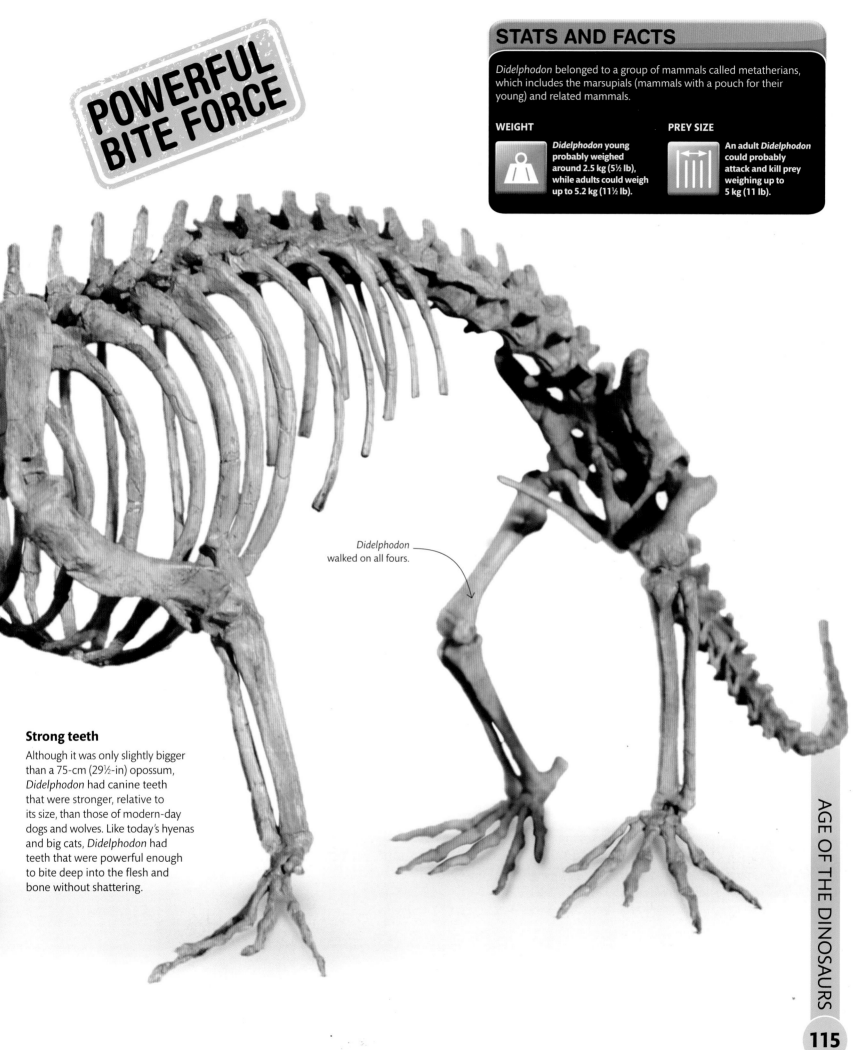

POWERFUL BITE FORCE

STATS AND FACTS

Didelphodon belonged to a group of mammals called metatherians, which includes the marsupials (mammals with a pouch for their young) and related mammals.

WEIGHT

Didelphodon young probably weighed around 2.5 kg (5½ lb), while adults could weigh up to 5.2 kg (11½ lb).

PREY SIZE

An adult *Didelphodon* could probably attack and kill prey weighing up to 5 kg (11 lb).

Didelphodon walked on all fours.

Strong teeth

Although it was only slightly bigger than a 75-cm (29½-in) opossum, *Didelphodon* had canine teeth that were stronger, relative to its size, than those of modern-day dogs and wolves. Like today's hyenas and big cats, *Didelphodon* had teeth that were powerful enough to bite deep into the flesh and bone without shattering.

AGE OF THE DINOSAURS

MONSTER CROC
DEINOSUCHUS

Related to but probably much larger than modern-day alligators and caimans, *Deinosuchus* was a gigantic, semiaquatic hunter. This powerful predator lurked in the estuaries and coastal waters of the ancient Western Interior Seaway during the Cretaceous Period. Most of what is known about *Deinosuchus* comes from the remains of a few fragments, which have been used to reconstruct its skeleton. This has made it tricky for paleontologists to estimate its size, but most agree that it could have been as large as 6–8 m (20–26 ft), with perhaps the oldest and largest individuals reaching 10 m (33 ft) in length.

Rows of bony plates lined the back, providing *Deinosuchus* protection from predators.

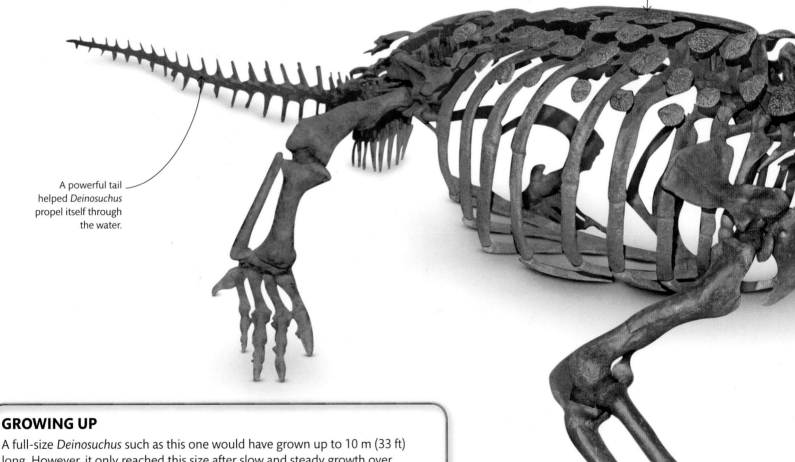

A powerful tail helped *Deinosuchus* propel itself through the water.

GROWING UP

A full-size *Deinosuchus* such as this one would have grown up to 10 m (33 ft) long. However, it only reached this size after slow and steady growth over several decades, with youngsters growing up to 30 cm (12 in) every year. Modern crocodylians, on the other hand, grow rapidly as hatchlings, then at a slower rate as they get older.

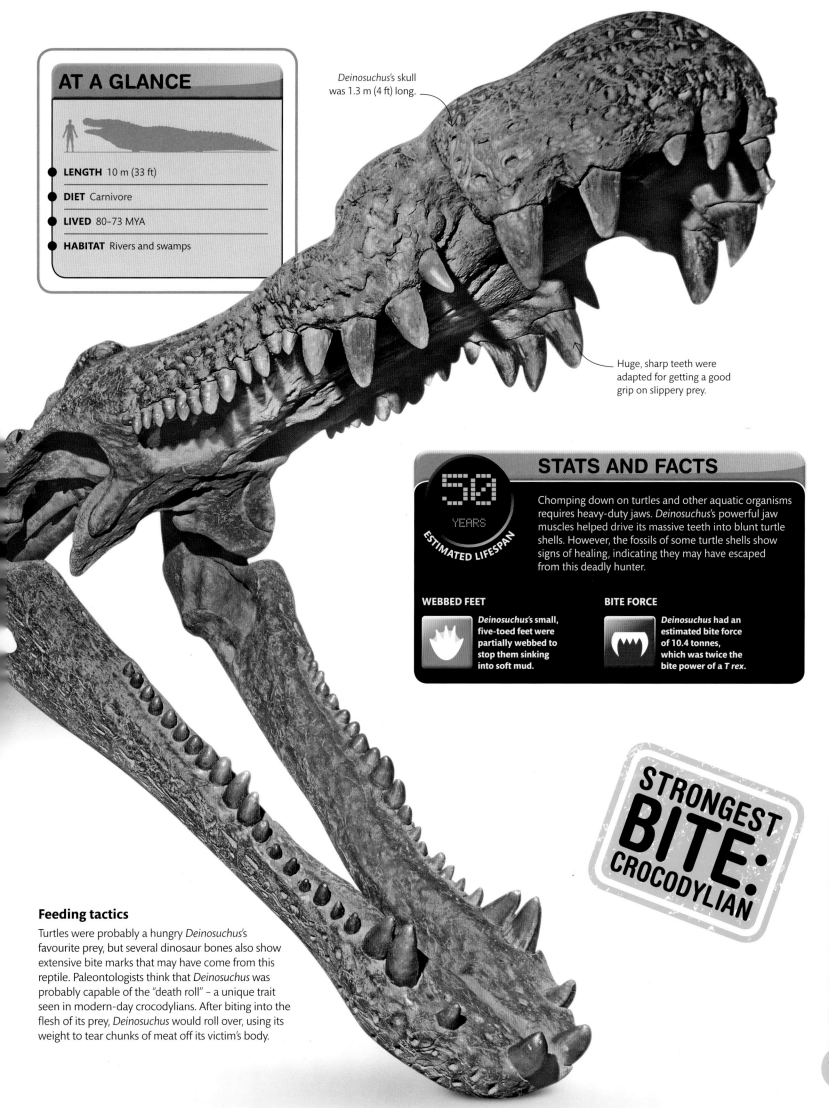

LENGTH 10 m (33 ft)

DIET Carnivore

LIVED 80–73 MYA

HABITAT Rivers and swamps

Deinosuchus's skull was 1.3 m (4 ft) long.

Huge, sharp teeth were adapted for getting a good grip on slippery prey.

STATS AND FACTS

50 YEARS ESTIMATED LIFESPAN

Chomping down on turtles and other aquatic organisms requires heavy-duty jaws. *Deinosuchus's* powerful jaw muscles helped drive its massive teeth into blunt turtle shells. However, the fossils of some turtle shells show signs of healing, indicating they may have escaped from this deadly hunter.

WEBBED FEET

Deinosuchus's small, five-toed feet were partially webbed to stop them sinking into soft mud.

BITE FORCE

Deinosuchus had an estimated bite force of 10.4 tonnes, which was twice the bite power of a *T rex*.

STRONGEST BITE: CROCODYLIAN

Feeding tactics

Turtles were probably a hungry *Deinosuchus's* favourite prey, but several dinosaur bones also show extensive bite marks that may have come from this reptile. Paleontologists think that *Deinosuchus* was probably capable of the "death roll" – a unique trait seen in modern-day crocodylians. After biting into the flesh of its prey, *Deinosuchus* would roll over, using its weight to tear chunks of meat off its victim's body.

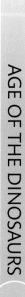

LARGEST DINOSAUR

Conifers probably made up a large portion of *Argentinosaurus's* diet.

A baby *Argentinosaurus* was so small that it could easily get crushed under a fully grown adult's feet.

STATS AND FACTS

Argentinosaurus probably ate up to 230 kg (500 lb) of food every day. The largest herbivore alive today, the African savanna elephant, only eats 136 kg (300 lb) of food in a day.

SPEED

The top walking speed of *Argentinosaurus* was probably 8 km/h (5 mph).

km/h		5		10
mph	3			6

A human walks at an average speed of 5.6 km/h (3½ mph).

LENGTH OF THIGH BONE

2.5 M (8 FT)

Small start

Several nesting sites containing the fossilized eggs of sauropods such as *Argentinosaurus* have been discovered in Argentina. They reveal that *Argentinosaurus* hatchlings were quite small, but that they grew rapidly. However, the babies probably received no parental care, and had to fend for themselves from the moment they hatched.

Argentinosaurus's pillar-like limbs and huge stumpy feet supported the weight of its massive body.

The creature's long neck allowed it to feed on vegetation other dinosaurs could not reach.

COLOSSAL PLANT-EATER
ARGENTINOSAURUS

There are many contenders for the title of largest and heaviest animal ever to walk the Earth, including the titanosaurs *Patagotitan* and *Notocolossus*, but the biggest of these gigantic beasts was probably *Argentinosaurus*. Although it is only known from a few fossil bones, paleontologists believe that this giant creature dwarfed many other dinosaurs of its time, and weighed around 80 tonnes. In order to satisfy its large appetite, *Argentinosaurus* tramped across the arid plains of modern-day South America in an endless search for vegetation.

HUNGRY HERD

Argentinosaurus, one of the largest land animals that has ever lived, had a huge appetite. Herds like this one would march across floodplains on a constant lookout for vegetation. The fossils of sauropod tracks show some species may have travelled in mixed-age herds. However, there is also evidence to suggest that adults and youngsters formed separate groups.

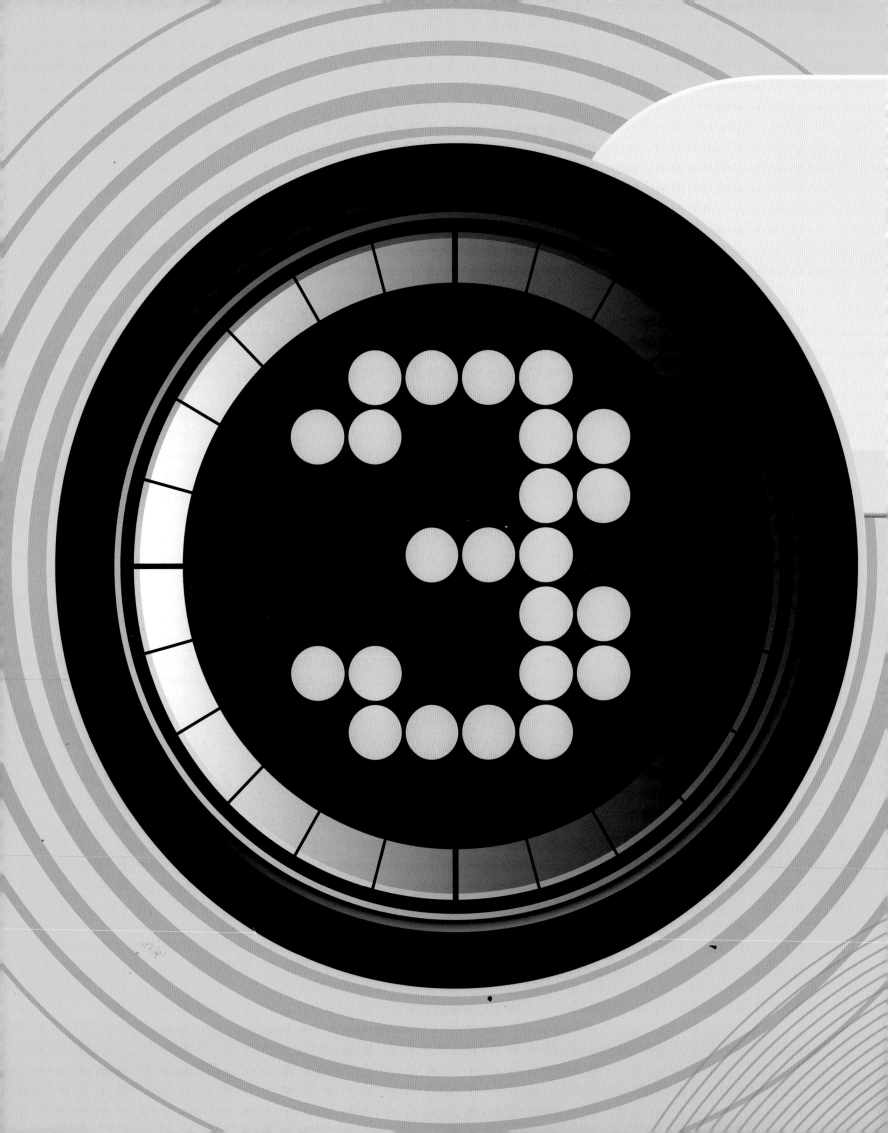

AFTER THE DINOSAURS

The era we live in today, the Cenozoic, began 66 million years ago with the extinction of many of the dominant reptile groups on land, in the air, and in the seas. This event opened up space for animals such as birds and mammals to occupy new habitats and adopt different lifestyles. A multitude of new species were about to evolve.

COLOSSAL SERPENT
TITANOBOA

The gigantic *Titanoboa* was one of the largest and heaviest snakes to have ever lived. Evolving around 6 million years after the extinction event that ended the Cretaceous Period, this relative of modern-day boa constrictors was probably a top predator in its time. Fossils of *Titanoboa* were first discovered in a coal mine in Colombia in 2009 and paleontologists have only found a few bones of this snake. The fossils tell us that *Titanoboa* had a large, bulky body. Like modern-day snakes, it probably had flexible jaws that helped it swallow large prey whole.

STATS AND FACTS

By comparing *Titanoboa*'s fossils to the bones of modern snakes, scientists estimate that it may have weighed 1,135 kg (2,502 lb) – more than 10 times as much as most modern anacondas and around four times as much as most modern zebras.

SKULL SIZE

The skull of *Titanoboa* was 40 cm (16 in) long – about three times the length of a modern reticulated python's skull.

WIDTH

The thickest parts of *Titanoboa*'s body were as wide as 1 m (3 ft), which is the average height of an eight-year-old child.

BIGGEST SNAKE

Titanoboa probably moved slowly, using its belly muscles to move in wavelike motions.

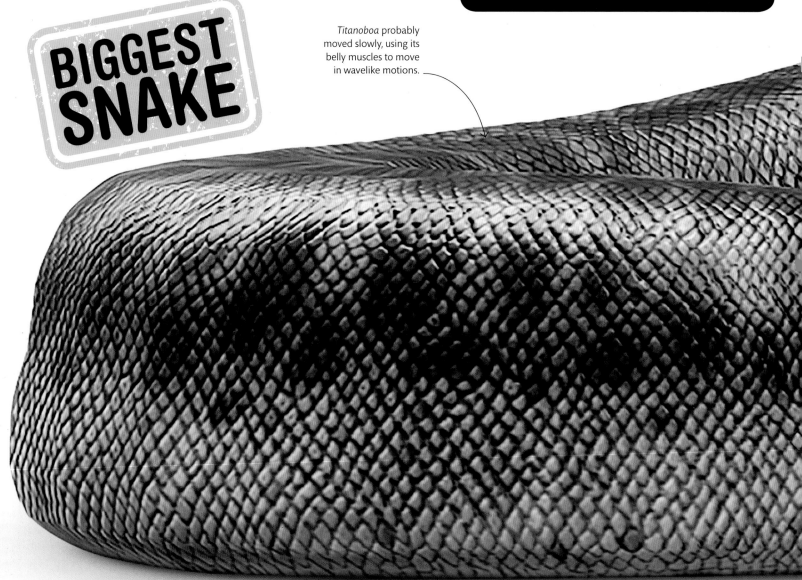

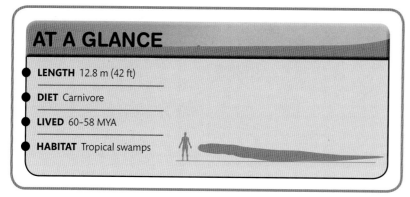

AT A GLANCE

- **LENGTH** 12.8 m (42 ft)
- **DIET** Carnivore
- **LIVED** 60–58 MYA
- **HABITAT** Tropical swamps

Aquatic predator

Titanoboa was probably an ambush predator, sneaking up on animals that came near the waterways in which it lurked. Coiling around its victim, *Titanoboa* may have used its strong trunk muscles to grip and slowly suffocate its prey. Numerous, closely packed teeth lined *Titanoboa's* jaws, perhaps indicating that its diet was made up mainly of large, slippery fish.

GIANT BONES

By studying the fossilized vertebrae (back bones) of *Titanoboa*, paleontologists have been able to estimate its enormous size. Measuring about 12.7 cm (5 in) in diameter, each vertebra was so large that it dwarfed the back bones of an adult anaconda (shown in front), the largest snake alive today.

Titanoboa probably shed its skin in one go, like modern snakes.

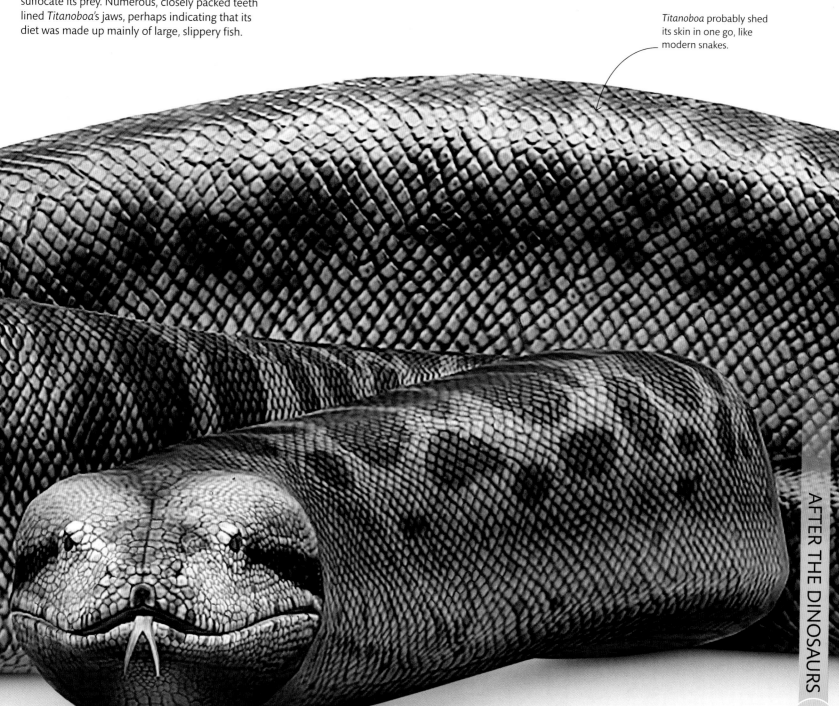

FLIGHTLESS GIANT
DROMORNIS

Although the massive prehistoric bird _Dromornis_ evolved from ancestors that could fly, it was flightless – its large, bulky frame was built for power rather than speed. _Dromornis_ had a powerful beak, which it probably used to forage for fruit, nuts, and foliage, and a large gut that helped it digest plant matter. This bird was once thought to be a relative of modern emus and ostriches, but recent research has shown it to be more closely related to waterfowl, such as ducks and geese.

Strong beak

Youngsters were probably covered in soft, downy feathers.

AT A GLANCE

- **HEIGHT** 3 m (10 ft)
- **DIET** Herbivore
- **LIVED** 8 MYA
- **HABITAT** Subtropical open woodlands

STATS AND FACTS

The Australian *Dromornis* was once hailed as the largest bird to have ever lived. However, it recently lost the top spot after the discovery of *Vorombe*, a giant prehistoric bird from Madagascar.

Dromornis males weighed about 584 kg (1,287 lb).

Vorombe had an average weight of 650 kg (1,433 lb).

At 156 kg (344 lb), the ostrich is the heaviest bird alive today.

Family values

Dromornis is thought to have had only a few chicks at a time, each of which grew slowly. Although *Dromornis* mothers nurtured the eggs before hatching, it is likely that both parents looked after the young. This bird aggressively defended its nests and, based on the behaviour of its living relatives, paleontologists think that *Dromornis* parents might have formed long-lasting pairs.

JAWS OF DEATH
OTODUS

Menacing every ocean on Earth, *Otodus* was a terrifyingly large shark. Commonly referred to by its species name, *megalodon*, *Otodus* had huge jaws lined with razor-sharp teeth that made it a formidable ocean hunter. Scientists think it may have gone extinct in part due to the presence of a famous marine predator that prowls modern-day oceans: the great white shark. Evolving around the same time as *Otodus*, the great white probably outcompeted young *Otodus* sharks for food, driving the larger species towards extinction.

AT A GLANCE

- **LENGTH** 10–18 m (33–59 ft)
- **DIET** Carnivore
- **LIVED** 15.9–3.2 MYA
- **HABITAT** Oceans

STRONGEST BITE: SHARK

STATS AND FACTS

Otodus's large size meant it had a monstrous bite force. Scientists think that the bone-crushing bite of this predator was likely to be 10 times stronger than that of the great white shark – the most powerful predatory shark alive today.

WEIGHT

An adult *Otodus* may have weighed as much as 50 tonnes.

SPEED

Otodus could swim at around 18 km/h (11 mph), which is a similar speed to some modern whales.

Killer teeth

Otodus was so large that it could easily prey on smaller whales. Whale bone fossils have been found bearing this giant's bite marks, including a vertebra (back bone) pierced by one of the predator's teeth.

RENEWABLE CHOMPERS

Otodus's teeth were around three times the size of the teeth of modern great white sharks, reaching up to 18 cm (7 in) in length. These robust teeth were continuously shed and replaced by new teeth throughout *Otodus*'s life. This renewal has made fossils of its teeth relatively common.

Great white shark tooth   ***Otodus* tooth**

As in other sharks, *Otodus*'s jaws projected outwards to seize prey.

SUPER SHARK

Looking for a quick snack, a hungry *Otodus* shark speeds towards a sea turtle. The turtle tries to defend itself by turning its hard, bony shell towards the deadly predator – a defensive move also seen in modern-day turtles. However, *Otodus* possesses one of the strongest bites in the animal kingdom, more than capable of piercing shell and bone, and the chances of this little turtle surviving look very slim.

The animal's tusks were extended upper incisors – in humans, these are the two front teeth.

Powerful jaw muscles helped *M borsoni* grind down its fibrous plant food.

LONGEST TUSKS

TOOTHED TITAN
MAMMUT BORSONI

Remains of the gigantic *Mammut borsoni* – one of the largest mammals ever to walk on land – suggest it could have reached a weight of 16 tonnes, which would make it heavier than some of the giant sauropods. Like modern-day elephants, *M borsoni* was a herbivore, and every day it would have ground down vast quantities of tough vegetation with its massive molar teeth. Its huge tusks are the longest ever known. Fossils of this animal have been unearthed at sites in Asia, Africa, Europe, and North America. One specimen discovered in Greece had particularly large tusks, at a record-breaking length of 5 m (16½ ft).

STATS AND FACTS

Although *Mammut borsoni* is a contender for the crown of "largest land mammal", some animals, such as its cousin *Palaeoloxodon* and the rhino-relative *Paraceratherium*, might have been bigger.

LIFESPAN

Like modern-day elephants, *M borsoni* may have lived for up to 71 years.

ORIGIN

M borsoni first appeared in what is now Europe, before it migrated to Asia.

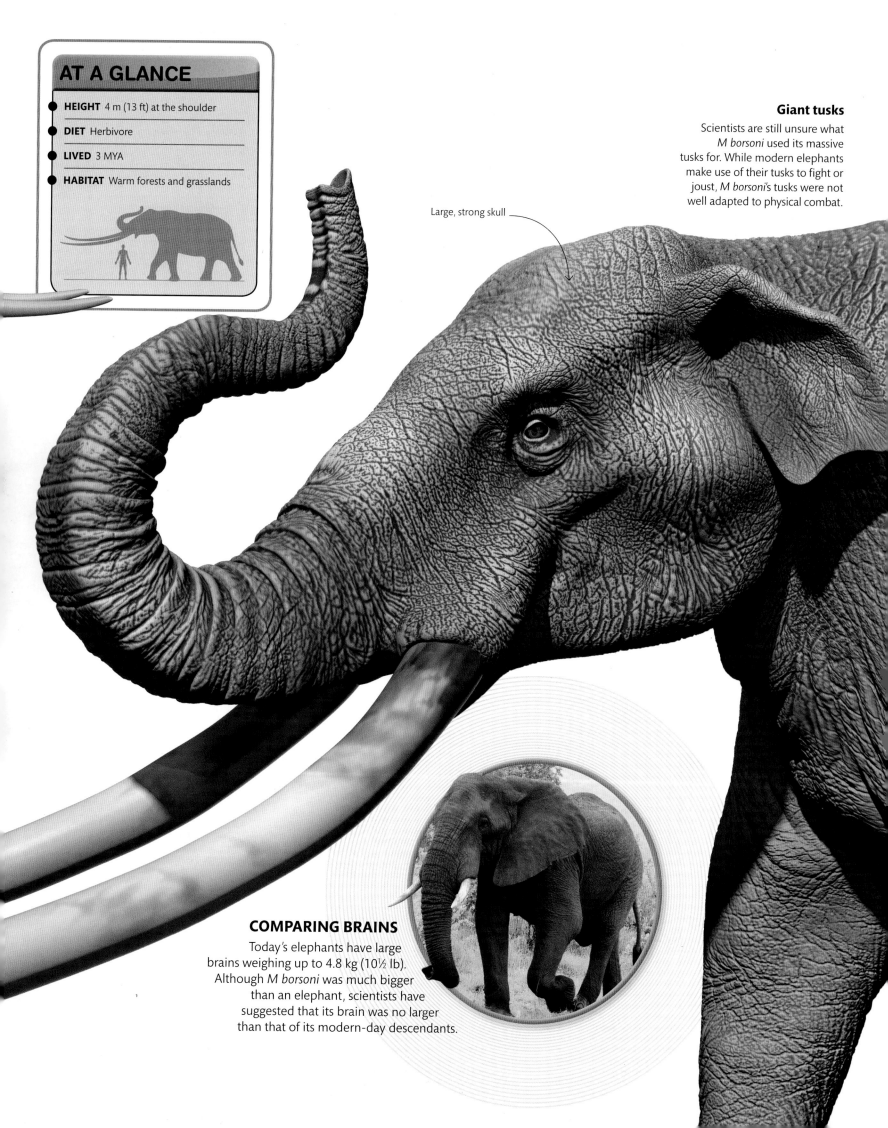

AT A GLANCE

- **HEIGHT** 4 m (13 ft) at the shoulder
- **DIET** Herbivore
- **LIVED** 3 MYA
- **HABITAT** Warm forests and grasslands

Giant tusks

Scientists are still unsure what *M borsoni* used its massive tusks for. While modern elephants make use of their tusks to fight or joust, *M borsoni*'s tusks were not well adapted to physical combat.

Large, strong skull

COMPARING BRAINS

Today's elephants have large brains weighing up to 4.8 kg (10½ lb). Although *M borsoni* was much bigger than an elephant, scientists have suggested that its brain was no larger than that of its modern-day descendants.

MIGHTY TUSKS
MAMMUTHUS

An extinct relative of modern-day elephants, *Mammuthus* once roamed the grasslands of the northern hemisphere, sharing its habitat with early humans. The best-known species was *Mammuthus primigenius*, or the woolly mammoth. This animal only became extinct relatively recently, with a small population surviving on an Arctic island up until just 4,000 years ago. Paleontologists have found several specimens of both calves and adults that were very well preserved thanks to the frosty environment in which they lived and died. As a result, this prehistoric creature is well studied.

AT A GLANCE

- **HEIGHT** 3.4 m (11 ft)
- **DIET** Herbivore
- **LIVED** 200,000–4,000 YA
- **HABITAT** Grasslands

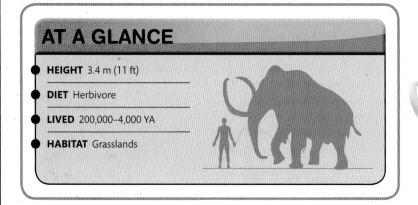

The woolly mammoth's long, curved tusks were probably used for display, competing for mates, and to brush snow off the grass before eating it.

COAT CLUES
Paleontologists have obtained strands of hair from mammoth fossils that tell us that these creatures were covered in thick, dark brown or blonde fur. Their coats would have kept them warm as they lumbered around their cold habitat.

Grass eater
Studies done on woolly mammoth teeth have revealed that their diet consisted of tough grasses. During the lean winter months, when vegetation was scarce, fat stores inside their bodies would have kept them going.

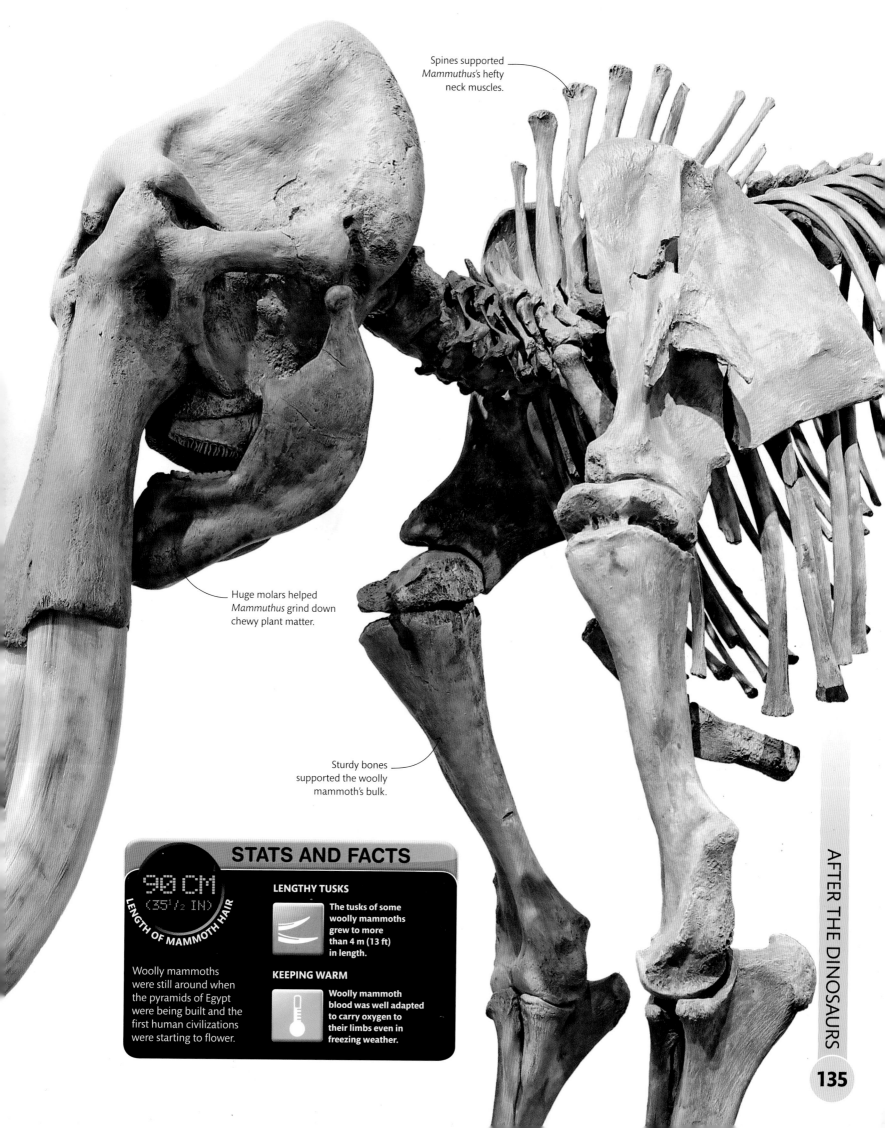

Spines supported
Mammuthus's hefty
neck muscles.

Huge molars helped
Mammuthus grind down
chewy plant matter.

Sturdy bones
supported the woolly
mammoth's bulk.

STATS AND FACTS

90 CM
(35¹/₂ IN)
LENGTH OF MAMMOTH HAIR

Woolly mammoths
were still around when
the pyramids of Egypt
were being built and the
first human civilizations
were starting to flower.

LENGTHY TUSKS

The tusks of some
woolly mammoths
grew to more
than 4 m (13 ft)
in length.

KEEPING WARM

Woolly mammoth
blood was well adapted
to carry oxygen to
their limbs even in
freezing weather.

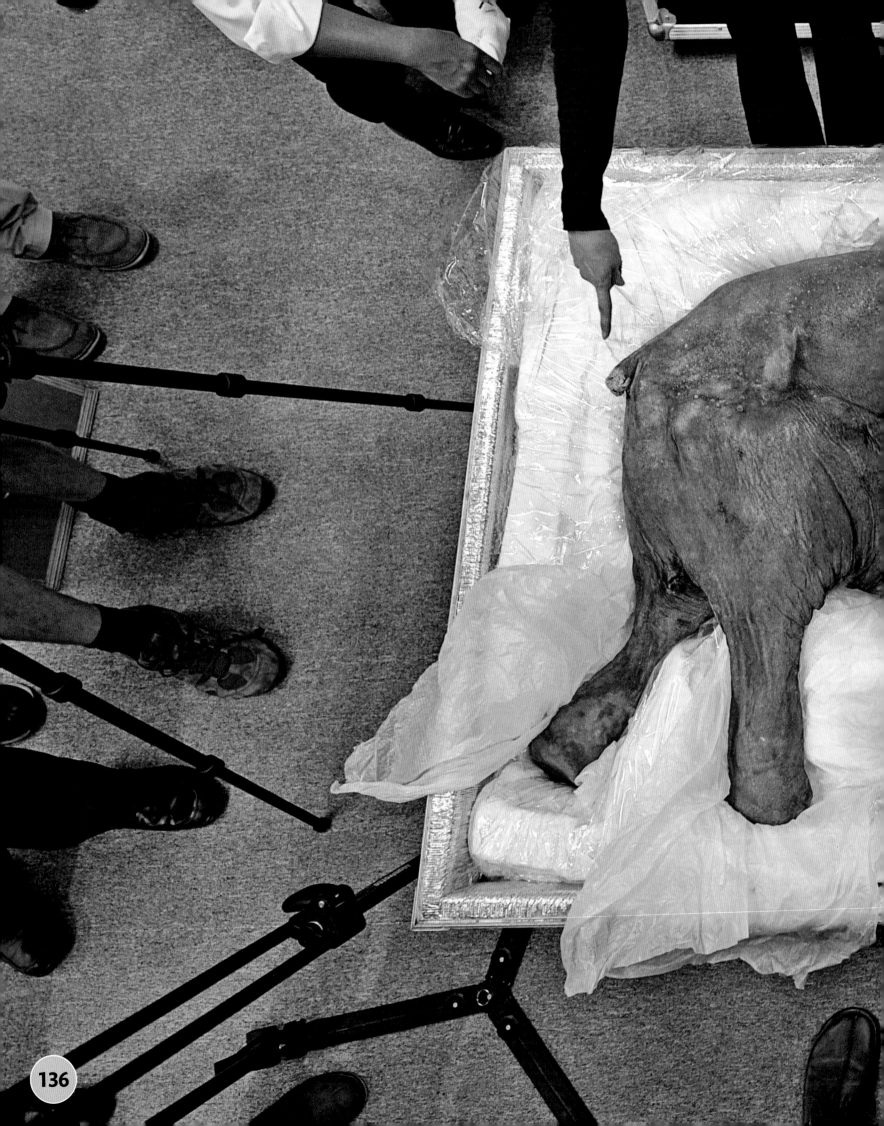

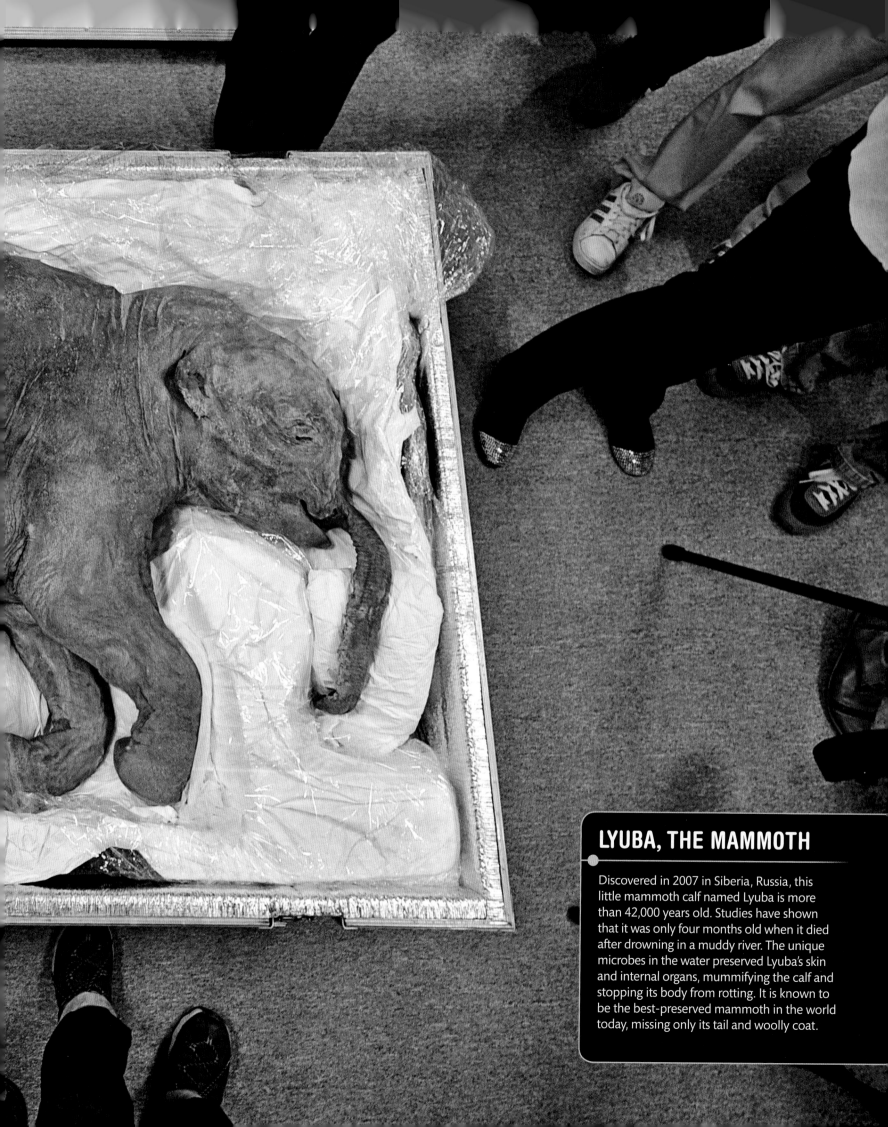

LYUBA, THE MAMMOTH

Discovered in 2007 in Siberia, Russia, this little mammoth calf named Lyuba is more than 42,000 years old. Studies have shown that it was only four months old when it died after drowning in a muddy river. The unique microbes in the water preserved Lyuba's skin and internal organs, mummifying the calf and stopping its body from rotting. It is known to be the best-preserved mammoth in the world today, missing only its tail and woolly coat.

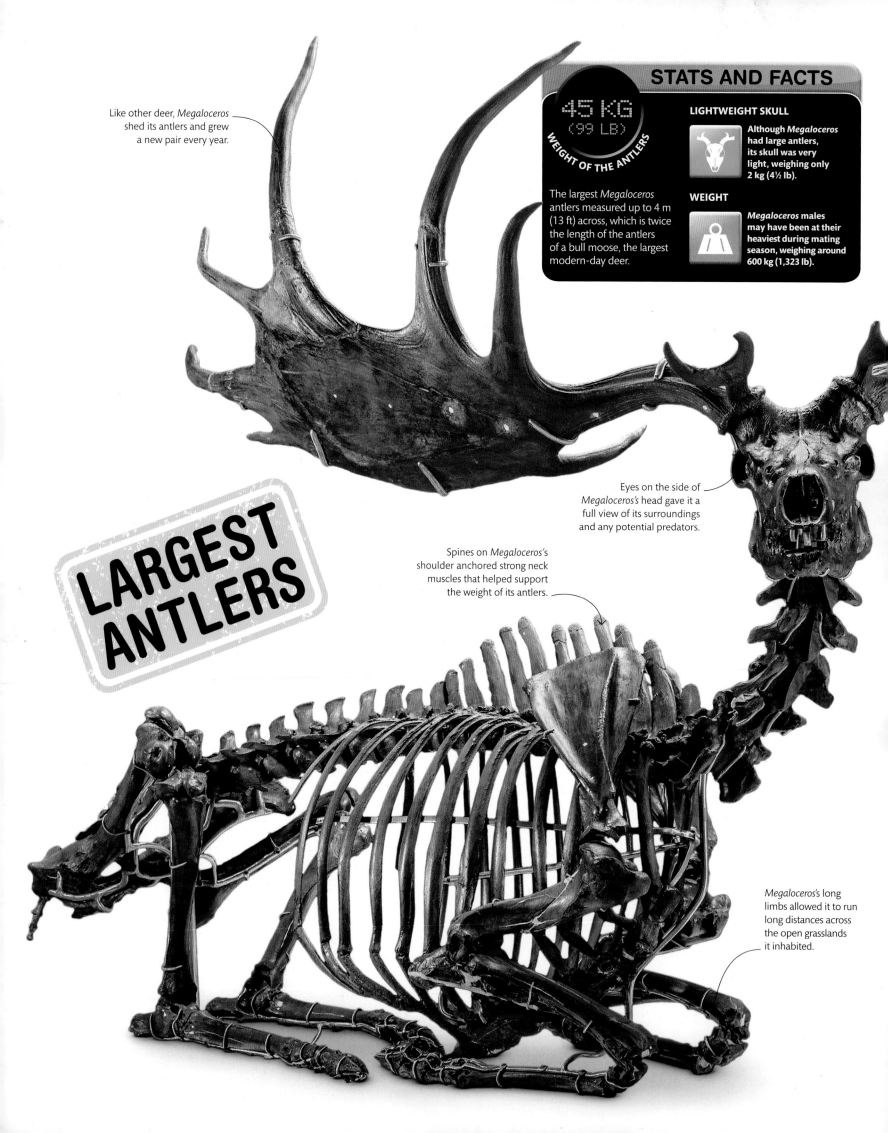

Like other deer, *Megaloceros* shed its antlers and grew a new pair every year.

The largest *Megaloceros* antlers measured up to 4 m (13 ft) across, which is twice the length of the antlers of a bull moose, the largest modern-day deer.

STATS AND FACTS

45 KG
(99 LB)
WEIGHT OF THE ANTLERS

LIGHTWEIGHT SKULL
Although *Megaloceros* had large antlers, its skull was very light, weighing only 2 kg (4½ lb).

WEIGHT
Megaloceros males may have been at their heaviest during mating season, weighing around 600 kg (1,323 lb).

Eyes on the side of *Megaloceros's* head gave it a full view of its surroundings and any potential predators.

Spines on *Megaloceros's* shoulder anchored strong neck muscles that helped support the weight of its antlers.

LARGEST ANTLERS

Megaloceros's long limbs allowed it to run long distances across the open grasslands it inhabited.

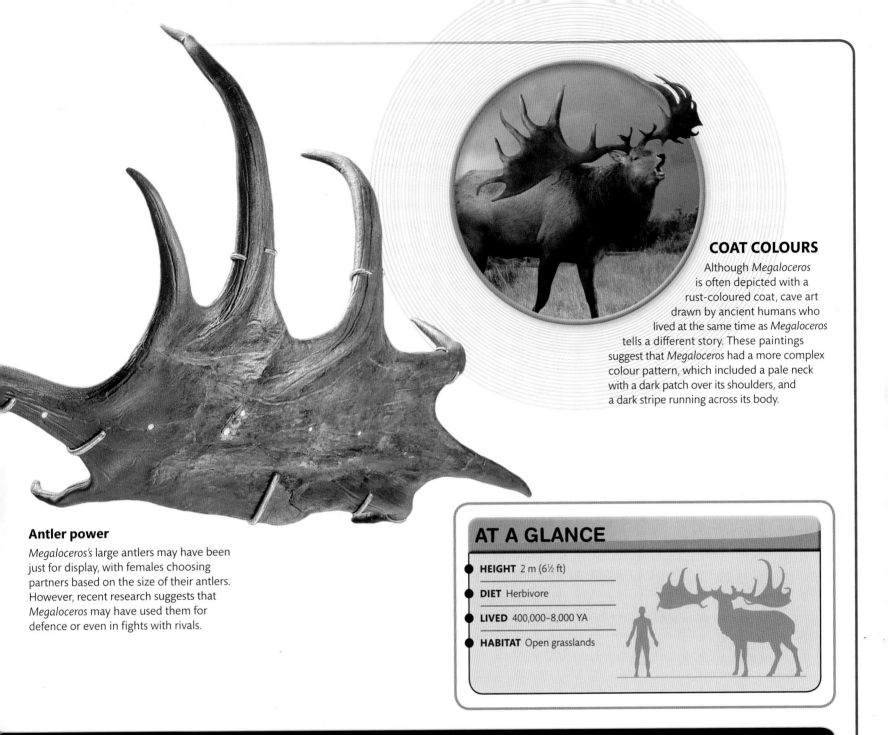

COAT COLOURS

Although *Megaloceros* is often depicted with a rust-coloured coat, cave art drawn by ancient humans who lived at the same time as *Megaloceros* tells a different story. These paintings suggest that *Megaloceros* had a more complex colour pattern, which included a pale neck with a dark patch over its shoulders, and a dark stripe running across its body.

Antler power

Megaloceros's large antlers may have been just for display, with females choosing partners based on the size of their antlers. However, recent research suggests that *Megaloceros* may have used them for defence or even in fights with rivals.

AT A GLANCE

- **HEIGHT** 2 m (6½ ft)
- **DIET** Herbivore
- **LIVED** 400,000–8,000 YA
- **HABITAT** Open grasslands

AMAZING ANTLERS
MEGALOCEROS

Sporting impressive antlers, *Megaloceros* ranged across the grasslands of much of what is now Europe and Asia. Although it is also known as the Irish elk, *Megaloceros* was actually more closely related to the much smaller modern-day fallow deer. Paleontologists used to believe that *Megaloceros* went extinct because its large and awkward antlers would have made it difficult for the animal to move around or graze easily. However, scientists now think that several different reasons, including competition for food with other deer species and a gradual change in the temperature of its habitat, may have caused *Megaloceros's* extinction.

SOARING SEABIRD
PELAGORNIS

With the largest wingspan of any bird ever, *Pelagornis* soared over the ancient seas in search of its next meal. Its fossils show that it had small toothlike structures in its beak, which would have helped it to feed on fish and other small aquatic creatures. This prehistoric bird evolved around 40 million years after the extinction of the flying reptiles known as pterosaurs. Because *Pelagornis* had small legs relative to the size of its body, it was unable to take off when floating on the top of the water. Paleontologists think that it probably caught its prey by swooping close to the surface, or by stealing the catch of smaller sea-going birds.

AT A GLANCE

WINGSPAN 6–7 m (20–23 ft)

DIET Fish and small marine creatures

LIVED 28–25 MYA

HABITAT Coastlines

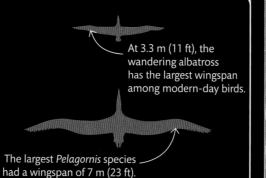

STATS AND FACTS

The toothlike structures in *Pelagornis*'s beak are called "pseudoteeth" (fake teeth), as they do not have the tough enamel covering found in the teeth of most animals. These are not present in the fossils of younger specimens, which suggests that babies may have been toothless and reliant on their parents for food.

At 3.3 m (11 ft), the wandering albatross has the largest wingspan among modern-day birds.

The largest *Pelagornis* species had a wingspan of 7 m (23 ft).

GLIDING HIGH

Like the modern-day albatross, *Pelagornis* was capable of cruising across the oceans at high altitudes for long periods of time, without settling on land. Research based on fossil finds suggests that despite its large size and heavy weight, it could glide at speeds of about 61 km/h (38 mph).

LARGEST
WINGSPAN: BIRD

SABRE-TOOTHED HUNTER
SMILODON

One of the top predators of its time, *Smilodon* is an ancient relative of today's cats. This giant feline preyed on deer and tapirs in forests across the region that is now the Americas, and is famous for the daggerlike canine teeth that it used to attack its prey. Many *Smilodon* fossils show wounds in the bones of the shoulders and back – a likely result of the creature ambushing its prey while hunting. Some skull fossils show puncture marks made by sabrelike canines, suggesting that these prehistoric cats may have even fought one another, with fatal consequences.

Ambush predator
Stalking through the undergrowth, *Smilodon* probably ambushed its victims by pouncing on them. It would then use its powerful arms to stop the struggling prey from moving too much, before delivering its fatal bites.

AT A GLANCE

- **LENGTH** 2.5 m (8 ft)
- **DIET** Carnivore
- **LIVED** 2.5–1 MYA
- **HABITAT** Forests and grasslands

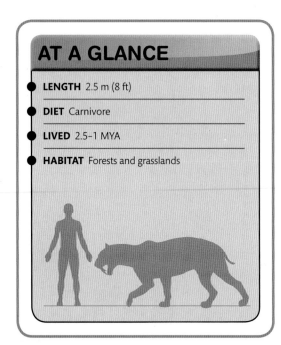

POWERFUL SKULL
Smilodon had a thick skull, which helped it deal with the impact of delivering a stabbing bite. It housed a pair of 28-cm (11-in) long canines that extended well below the lower jaws. These grew around 6 mm (⅕ in) per month, and stopped growing when *Smilodon* was a little over three years old.

Although *Smilodon* is usually shown with a patterned coat, paleontologists are uncertain whether this animal's coat was plain or patterned.

STATS AND FACTS

The smallest member of this genus, *Smilodon gracilis*, weighed around 75 kg (165 lb), while the largest, *Smilodon populator*, might have tipped the scales at 470 kg (1,036 lb).

In order to clear the huge canines, *Smilodon* could open its mouth by a whopping 120 degrees.

A yawning tiger can open its mouth by about 70 degrees.

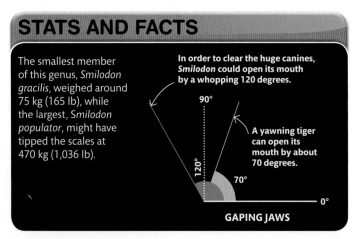

90°

120°

70°

0°

GAPING JAWS

KILLER
TEETH

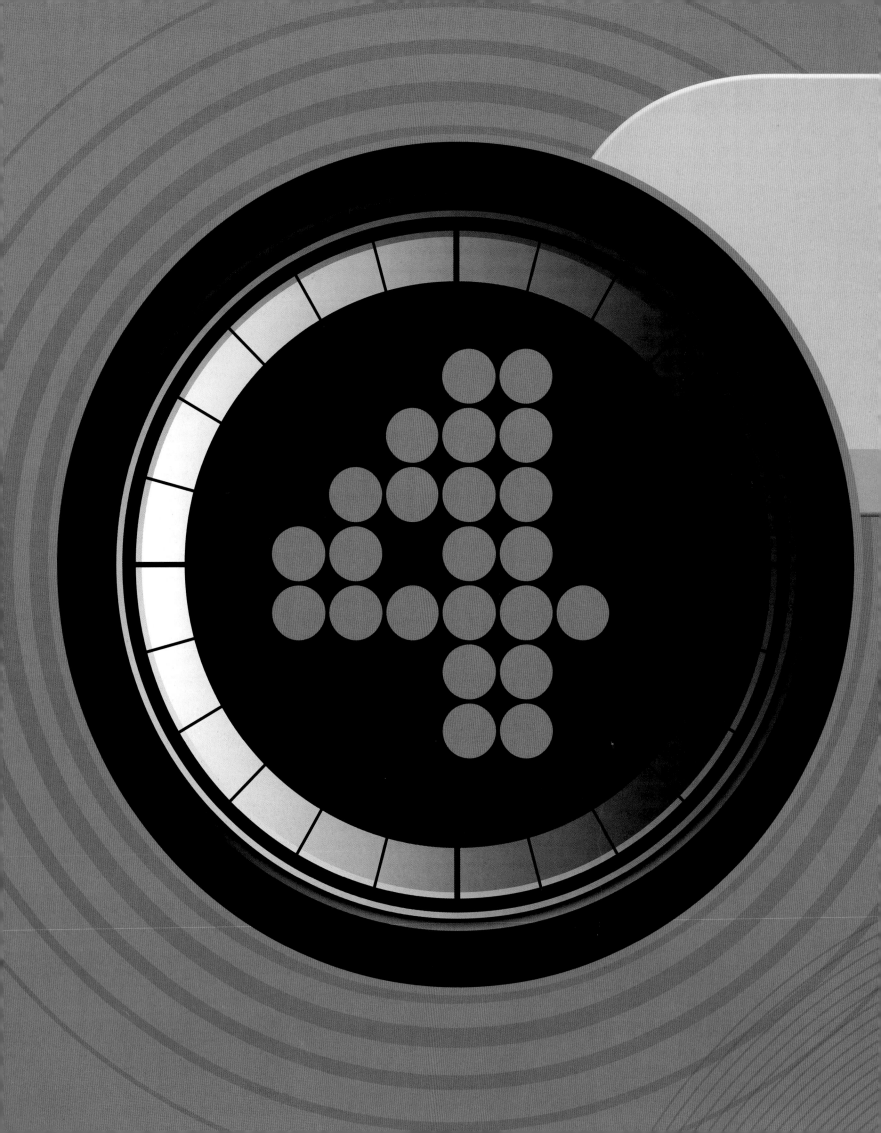

STUNNING SCIENCE

Scientists now have a huge range of technologies at their fingertips that allow them to study extinct animals in incredible detail, unlocking the secrets of their bones and even untangling information from their preserved soft tissues.

COLLISION COURSE
MASS EXTINCTION

When a 13-km (8-mile) wide asteroid crashed into Earth 66 million years ago, it left behind a 180-km (112-mile) wide crater, scarring the planet's crust. This impact caused one of the largest known mass extinctions, bringing the Cretaceous Period to an end as a wide range of species, including all the non-bird dinosaurs, disappeared from the face of Earth. The asteroid landed in a shallow sea and caused a tsunami, with waves 300 m (984 ft) high, that devastated low-lying regions. The dust and gases that were released into the atmosphere after the impact blocked out the Sun, causing the planet to cool down, which in turn led to the collapse of ecosystems on land and in the seas.

The outer layers of the asteroid produced a fiery glow as they burned up. The asteroid was travelling at a speed of 20 km per second (12 miles per second) when it entered Earth's atmosphere.

DECCAN TRAPS

Some scientists have suggested that massive volcanic eruptions in what is now central India may also have contributed to the extinction event. These volcanoes had been continuously erupting for just under a million years and the eruptions may have intensified as a result of the asteroid impact. The lava flow from the eruptions formed the layers of rock pictured here, which are known as the Deccan Traps.

Asteroid impact

When the asteroid crashed into Earth, it left its mark in the planet's rocks. A thin layer of sediment lies between the Late Cretaceous rocks and the more recent rocks from the Paleogene Period. This band of rock is called the Cretaceous–Paleogene (K-Pg) boundary. It is rich in iridium, an element that is rare on Earth but common in asteroids. This iridium may have been deposited as a cloud of dust after the asteroid hit Earth. Fossils of all non-bird dinosaurs are found in rocks below this thin boundary layer.

A huge number of gases were released into the atmosphere when the asteroid hit Earth's crust.

FEATHERED FIND
ARCHAEOPTERYX

The discovery of fossils of *Archaeopteryx* was one of the first finds to make paleontologists think that birds evolved from dinosaurs. Many even consider *Archaeopteryx* to be the first bird, capable of short bursts of flight. However, its fossils show that it also possessed similar traits to its theropod ancestors, including a bony tail and a jaw full of teeth. *Archaeopteryx* lived on a set of Late Jurassic islands in what is now Europe, and many well-preserved fossils have been found in a limestone quarry in Germany. The fossils are in such excellent condition because the creatures fell into prehistoric lagoons containing very salty water that preserved their delicate frames and soft tissues.

AT A GLANCE

YEAR OF DISCOVERY 1875

PLACE Germany

DISCOVERER Jakob Niemeyer

LIVED 150 MYA

FOSSILIZED FEATHER
Until 2018, this fossil feather was believed to belong to *Archaeopteryx*. However, recent research has shown that it belonged to a different feathered dinosaur, giving more evidence that dinosaurs didn't just have scaly skin.

ARCHAEOPTERYX

WORLD FAMOUS

This fossil is the most complete of all *Archaeopteryx* fossils discovered so far. Using high-powered imaging techniques, paleontologists have even found that the crow-sized *Archaeopteryx* had dull, black feathers.

COLOUR CLUES
MICRORAPTOR

In 2012, paleontologists made an exciting discovery while examining this excellently preserved fossil in northeastern China. This specimen, of *Microraptor*, was in such good condition that they were able to identify and even study pigments on soft tissues, such as feathers. This little theropod was closely related to modern birds, had four feathered "wings", and may have been capable of powered flight. The stomach area of one *Microraptor* fossil contained the fossil of another small animal, later identified as a new species of prehistoric lizard. This discovery also showed that *Microraptor* probably swallowed prey whole and head first, just as modern carnivorous birds do.

AT A GLANCE

- **YEAR OF RESEARCH** 2012
- **PLACE** China
- **STUDIED BY** Quanguo Li and team
- **LIVED** 125–120 MYA

UV DISCOVERIES

One of the techniques used to study *Microraptor*'s feathers involved shining ultraviolet (UV) light on the fossil. Certain parts of it appeared fluorescent under UV light (as seen here), which allowed scientists to study the extent and arrangement of fossilized soft tissue such as feathers.

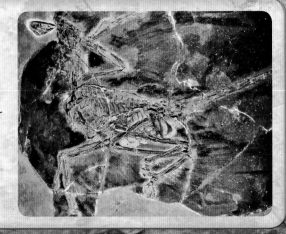

SHINY FEATHERS

The preserved pigments in the *Microraptor*'s fossilized feathers reveal it had iridescent black colouring similar to that of modern-day starlings. Such flashy feathers might have played a role in display, as they do in modern bird species.

MICRORAPTOR

Ancient bone bed

This fossil was found in Dinosaur Provincial Park, a famous location in Alberta, Canada, that is littered with the fossils of more than 50 dinosaur species. These fossils belong to animals that lived between 77 and 75.5 million years ago, and the specimens range from ornithomimids (such as this one) to hadrosaurs and ankylosaurs.

A long, slender neck helped *Struthiomimus* reach tall plants.

Struthiomimus's long arms would have been covered with feathers.

STRUTHIOMIMUS

A long, slender neck helped *Struthiomimus* reach tall plants.

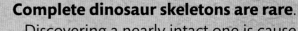
STRUTHIOMIMUS

The long tail on an ornithomimid such as *Struthiomimus* helped it balance its weight while running at high speed.

Complete dinosaur skeletons are rare. Discovering a nearly intact one is cause for celebration because complete specimens reveal much more about a dinosaur and how it might have lived than partial fragments can. This *Struthiomimus* skeleton is one of the most complete fossils ever found. *Struthiomimus* was an ornithomimid (a fast-moving, long-limbed theropod) that lived during the Late Cretaceous Period in what is now North America. This particular specimen was preserved in the "death pose", with the animal's neck bent back. Although many dinosaur fossils have been discovered in this pose, paleontologists are still unsure about the reasons for this strange position.

AT A GLANCE

- **YEAR OF DISCOVERY** 1914
- **PLACE** Alberta, Canada
- **FOUND BY** Barnum Brown
- **LIVED** 83–71 MYA

MR BONES

The American paleontologist Barnum Brown was an extraordinary fossil hunter. Known as "Mr Bones", he collected hundreds of specimens, including this *Struthiomimus* fossil. Although he is credited for the discovery of numerous dinosaurs, his most important find was the first ever set of *Tyrannosaurus* bones, in 1902.

DINO DUEL
VELOCIRAPTOR AND PROTOCERATOPS

Discovering two dinosaur fossils in the same rock is rare enough, but finding a fossil of two dinosaurs locked in combat is even more astounding. This one-in-a-million find shows a *Velociraptor* with its clawed foot lodged in a *Protoceratops*'s throat, while the *Protoceratops* crushes the *Velociraptor*'s arm in its beak. It was discovered by a Polish-Mongolian team of paleontologists in the early 1970s. Scientists think that this fossil may be evidence of the *Velociraptor* hunting the herbivore, or it may simply have chanced upon *Protoceratops* and startled it. Either way, both have been frozen in time for more than 71 million years.

AT A GLANCE

- **YEAR OF DISCOVERY** 1971
- **PLACE** Gobi Desert, Mongolia
- **FOUND BY** Halszka Osmolska and team
- **LIVED** 75–71 MYA

Serrated teeth

VELOCIRAPTOR
Velociraptor was a small theropod that inhabited the arid deserts of a region now in Mongolia. The arm fossils of a *Velociraptor* specimen show attachment sites for ligaments that may have held long feathers in place.

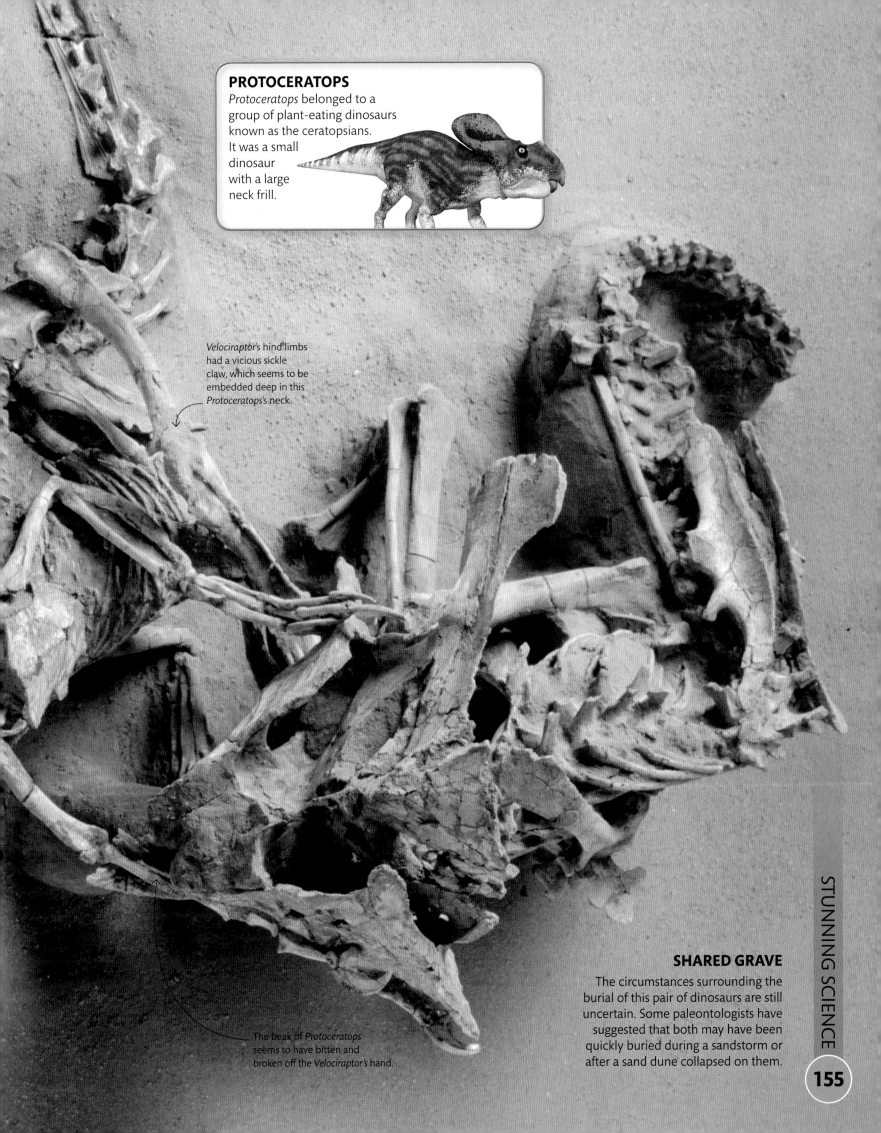

PROTOCERATOPS

Protoceratops belonged to a group of plant-eating dinosaurs known as the ceratopsians. It was a small dinosaur with a large neck frill.

Velociraptor's hind limbs had a vicious sickle claw, which seems to be embedded deep in this *Protoceratops*'s neck.

The beak of *Protoceratops* seems to have bitten and broken off the *Velociraptor*'s hand.

SHARED GRAVE

The circumstances surrounding the burial of this pair of dinosaurs are still uncertain. Some paleontologists have suggested that both may have been quickly buried during a sandstorm or after a sand dune collapsed on them.

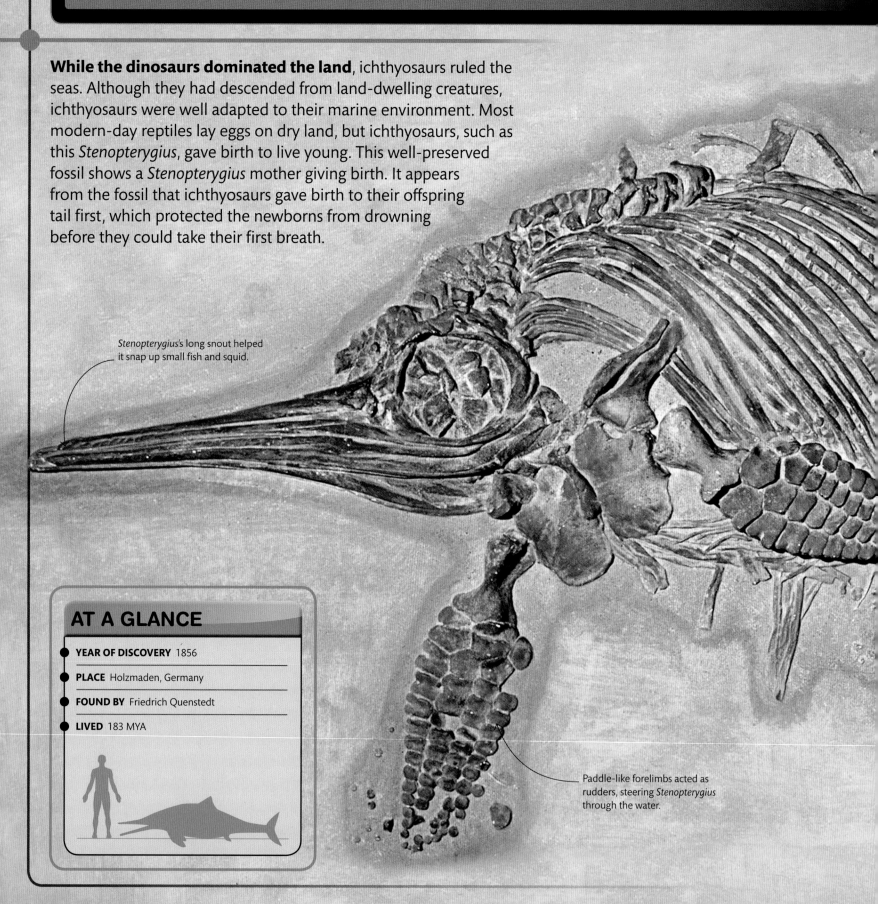

MOTHER AND BABY
STENOPTERYGIUS

While the dinosaurs dominated the land, ichthyosaurs ruled the seas. Although they had descended from land-dwelling creatures, ichthyosaurs were well adapted to their marine environment. Most modern-day reptiles lay eggs on dry land, but ichthyosaurs, such as this *Stenopterygius*, gave birth to live young. This well-preserved fossil shows a *Stenopterygius* mother giving birth. It appears from the fossil that ichthyosaurs gave birth to their offspring tail first, which protected the newborns from drowning before they could take their first breath.

Stenopterygius's long snout helped it snap up small fish and squid.

AT A GLANCE

- **YEAR OF DISCOVERY** 1856
- **PLACE** Holzmaden, Germany
- **FOUND BY** Friedrich Quenstedt
- **LIVED** 183 MYA

Paddle-like forelimbs acted as rudders, steering *Stenopterygius* through the water.

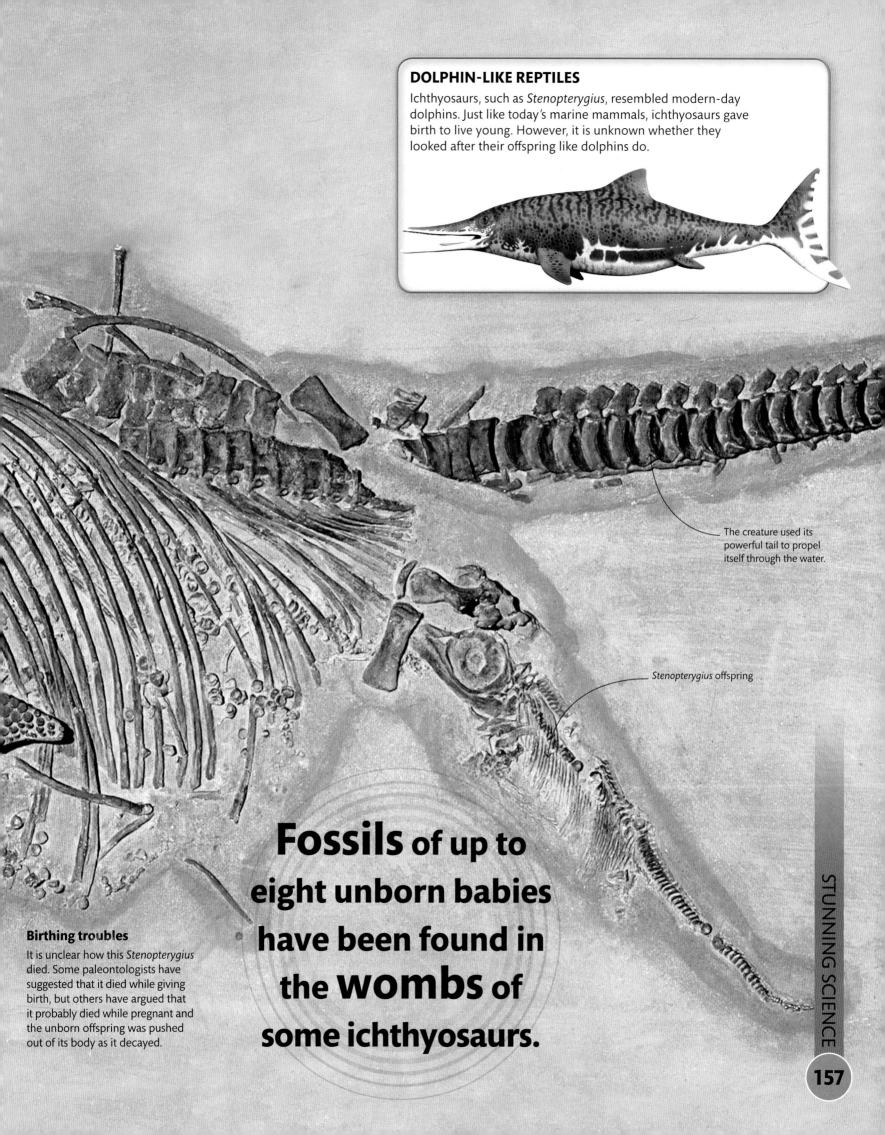

DOLPHIN-LIKE REPTILES
Ichthyosaurs, such as *Stenopterygius*, resembled modern-day dolphins. Just like today's marine mammals, ichthyosaurs gave birth to live young. However, it is unknown whether they looked after their offspring like dolphins do.

The creature used its powerful tail to propel itself through the water.

Stenopterygius offspring

Fossils of up to eight unborn babies have been found in the **wombs** of some ichthyosaurs.

Birthing troubles
It is unclear how this *Stenopterygius* died. Some paleontologists have suggested that it died while giving birth, but others have argued that it probably died while pregnant and the unborn offspring was pushed out of its body as it decayed.

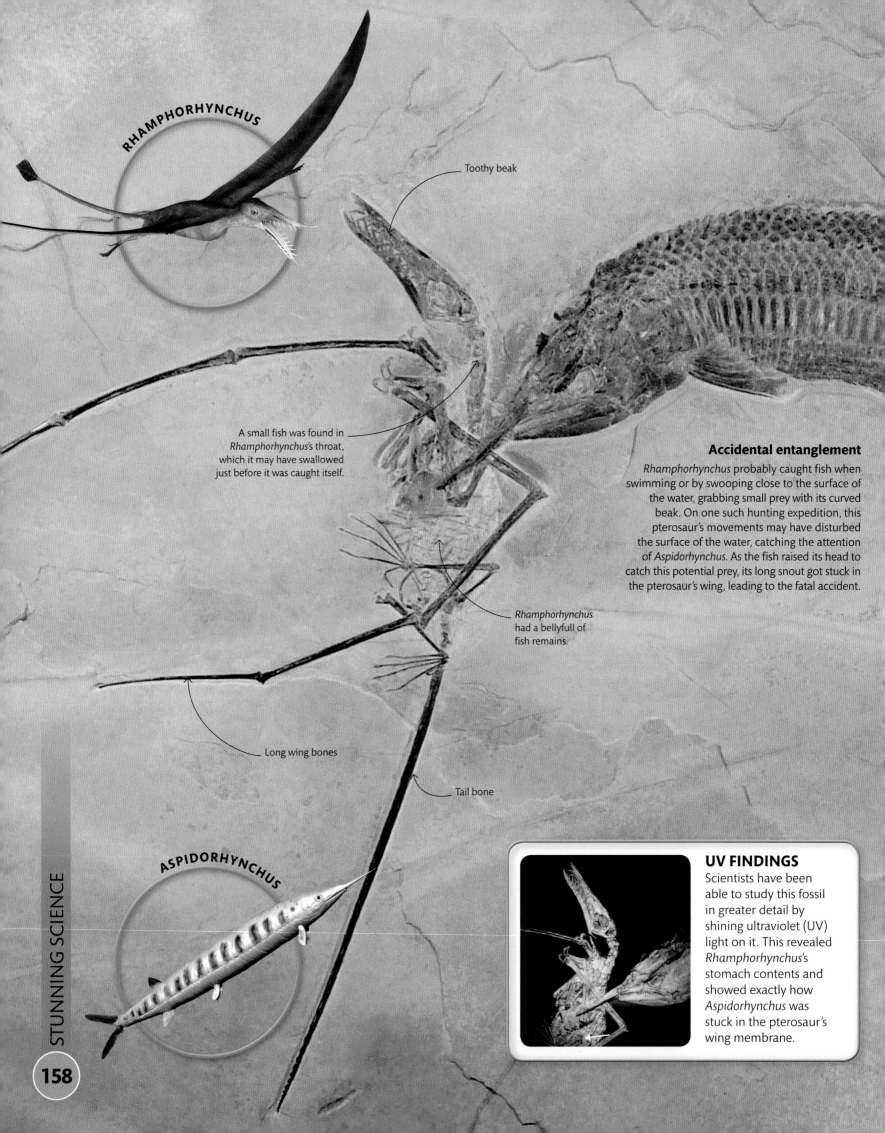

RHAMPHORHYNCHUS

Toothy beak

A small fish was found in
Rhamphorhynchus's throat,
which it may have swallowed
just before it was caught itself.

Accidental entanglement

Rhamphorhynchus probably caught fish when
swimming or by swooping close to the surface of
the water, grabbing small prey with its curved
beak. On one such hunting expedition, this
pterosaur's movements may have disturbed
the surface of the water, catching the attention
of *Aspidorhynchus*. As the fish raised its head to
catch this potential prey, its long snout got stuck in
the pterosaur's wing, leading to the fatal accident.

Rhamphorhynchus
had a bellyfull of
fish remains.

Long wing bones

Tail bone

ASPIDORHYNCHUS

UV FINDINGS

Scientists have been
able to study this fossil
in greater detail by
shining ultraviolet (UV)
light on it. This revealed
Rhamphorhynchus's
stomach contents and
showed exactly how
Aspidorhynchus was
stuck in the pterosaur's
wing membrane.

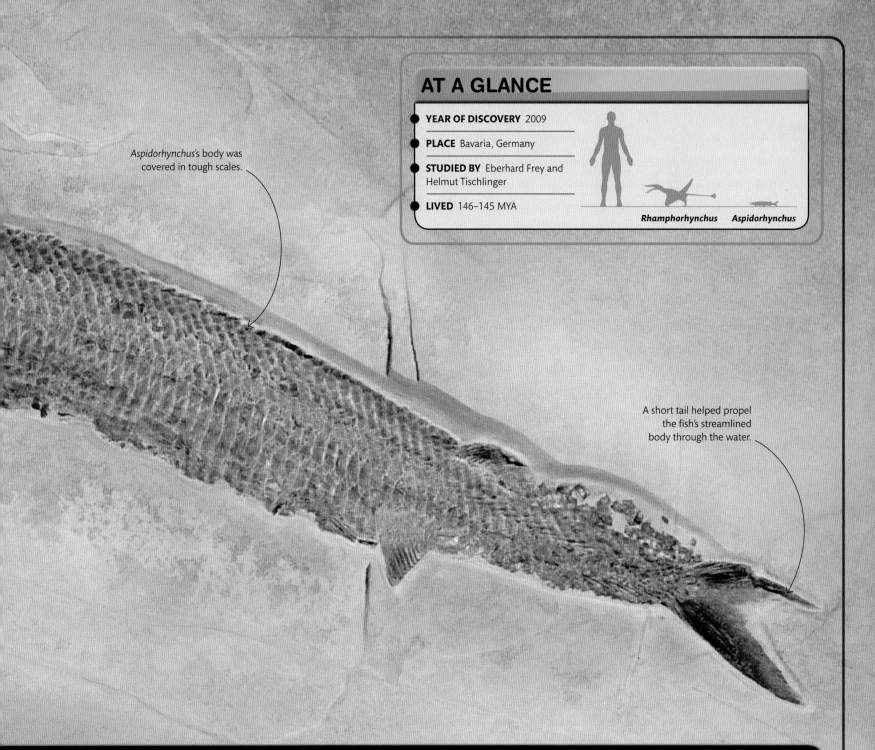

Aspidorhynchus's body was covered in tough scales.

A short tail helped propel the fish's streamlined body through the water.

AT A GLANCE

● **YEAR OF DISCOVERY** 2009

● **PLACE** Bavaria, Germany

● **STUDIED BY** Eberhard Frey and Helmut Tischlinger

● **LIVED** 146–145 MYA

Rhamphorhynchus   *Aspidorhynchus*

DEADLY ENCOUNTER
ASPIDORHYNCHUS AND RHAMPHORHYNCHUS

This encounter between the fish *Aspidorhynchus* and the pterosaur *Rhamphorhynchus* was very much a case of wrong place, wrong time. Found inside limestone rock in southern Germany, this incredible fossil perfectly captures a snapshot of Jurassic life. *Aspidorhynchus*'s large, pointed "bill" accidentally became entangled in the wing membrane of the pterosaur and despite repeated attempts to escape, the fish was unable to free itself. Both creatures sank to the bottom of a lagoon, where the oxygen-poor water suffocated and killed them.

PROTECTIVE PARENT

CITIPATI MOTHER

When several remarkable specimens of Citipati (a type of feathered dinosaur called an oviraptorosaur) were found with their eggs, experts made a link between these brooding dinosaurs and similar nesting behaviour of modern birds. More recently, however, scientists have begun to question this idea. The discovery of intact *Citipati* fossil nests that contained pairs of eggs arranged in three to four circles with a clear centre was unlike anything seen in modern animals.

The neck and skull of this *Citipati* were lost in the original fossil and later added on in the cast.

A small, hollow crest on *Citipati*'s skull was similar to the crests on modern-day cassowaries.

A long, flexible neck allowed *Citipati* to keep an eye out for predators in the distance.

Sitting tight

This cast of a *Citipati* in a nest shows how it laid its eggs in a circle with enough space for a parent to sit comfortably in the middle. Although this nest has 22 eggs, most complete nests have at least 30 eggs in them. Some scientists suggest that this specimen may be the father sitting with the eggs to protect them, while others think that it may be a mother who had not yet finished laying all her eggs when she died.

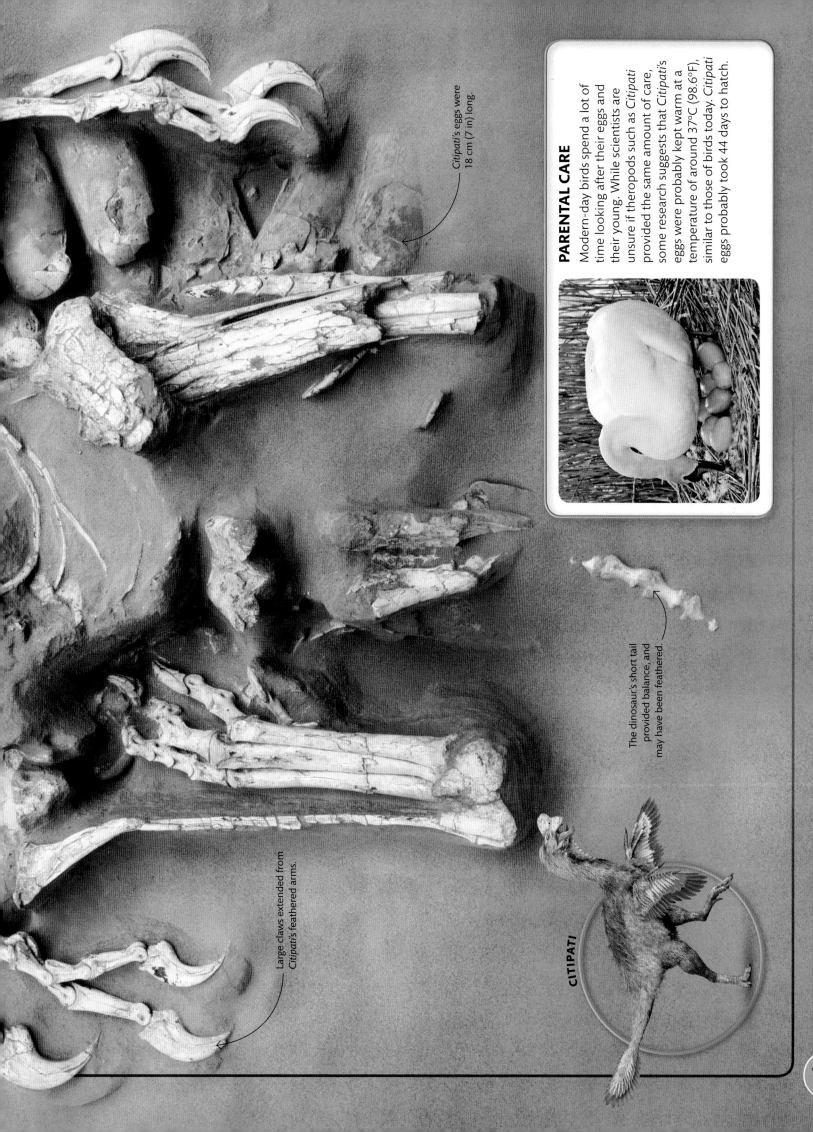

Citipati's eggs were 18 cm (7 in) long.

PARENTAL CARE

Modern-day birds spend a lot of time looking after their eggs and their young. While scientists are unsure if theropods such as Citipati provided the same amount of care, some research suggests that Citipati's eggs were probably kept warm at a temperature of around 37°C (98.6°F), similar to those of birds today. Citipati eggs probably took 44 days to hatch.

The dinosaur's short tail provided balance, and may have been feathered.

Large claws extended from Citipati's feathered arms.

CITIPATI

FOSSIL NEST

This fossilized nest was discovered in a Mongolian desert in the 1920s. Containing long, narrow eggs, this nest was initially believed to belong to *Protoceratops*. A fossilized theropod discovered near the nest was assumed to have died while trying to raid it, and was named *Oviraptor* – meaning "egg thief". However, further research revealed that the nest, in fact, belonged to the theropod, which probably died while tending to its eggs.

TIMELESS TRAILS

DINOSAUR FOOTPRINTS

Several thousand dinosaur footprints line the 100-m (328-ft) high walls of a limestone quarry in Cal Orcko, Bolivia. These prints were laid down by a range of different dinosaurs as they marched through the region's soft ground during the Late Cretaceous Period. Successive droughts and rainfalls helped to repeatedly dry and then cover these prints in mud, which fossilized and preserved them. Several million years later, movements in Earth's crust pushed the horizontal layers of rock upwards and sideways, creating this near-vertical wall that has been informally called the "dinosaur dance floor".

Theropod tracks cut across the long trail of sauropod footprints.

These sauropod tracks probably belonged to titanosaur.

Wall of prints

The prints on this wall were created around a prehistoric lake that attracted many herbivores who came to drink and feed, as well as the predators that hunted them. About 462 individual trackways have been traced across this 1.2-km (¾-mile) long slab of rock, providing valuable information about dinosaur sizes from the distance between their prints. This also allows scientists to estimate the speed at which these creatures walked.

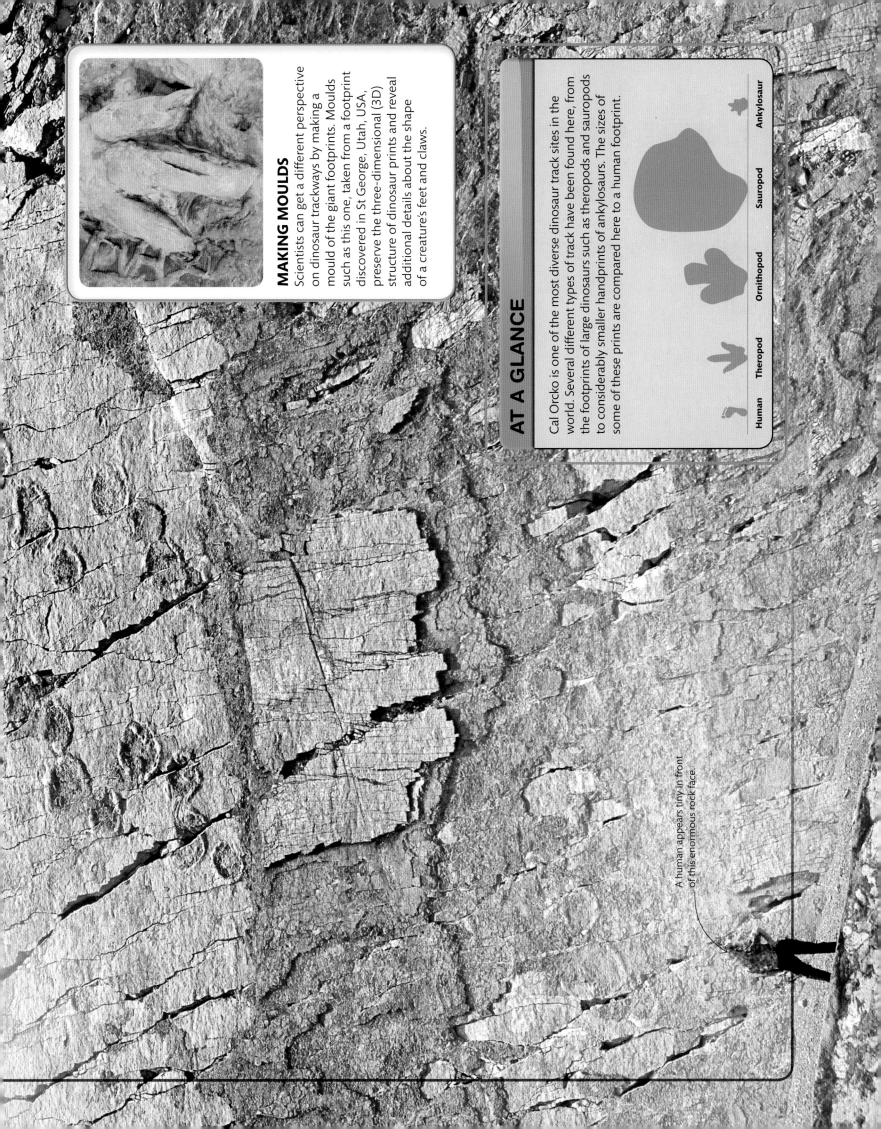

MAKING MOULDS

Scientists can get a different perspective on dinosaur trackways by making a mould of the giant footprints. Moulds such as this one, taken from a footprint discovered in St George, Utah, USA, preserve the three-dimensional (3D) structure of dinosaur prints and reveal additional details about the shape of a creature's feet and claws.

AT A GLANCE

Cal Orcko is one of the most diverse dinosaur track sites in the world. Several different types of track have been found here, from the footprints of large dinosaurs such as theropods and sauropods to considerably smaller handprints of ankylosaurs. The sizes of some of these prints are compared here to a human footprint.

Human	Theropod	Ornithopod	Sauropod	Ankylosaur

A human appears tiny in front of this enormous rock face.

This reconstructed skull is used in place of the creature's original skull, which was squashed during fossilization.

A gruelling task

It took many paleontologists a combined total of 30,000 hours to prepare "Sue" for display in a museum. While studying the skeleton, they found that "Sue" had suffered many injuries during the course of its life, including broken ribs, a damaged shoulder blade, and even holes in its skull.

"SUE" AND SUE

For 67 million years, the *T rex* "Sue" lay hidden in rock. It took a team of excavators, including Sue Hendrickson (pictured here), more than two weeks to chisel the specimen out of the stone. Scientists think that "Sue" may have been covered by water and mud soon after death so its remains were not scattered by scavengers.

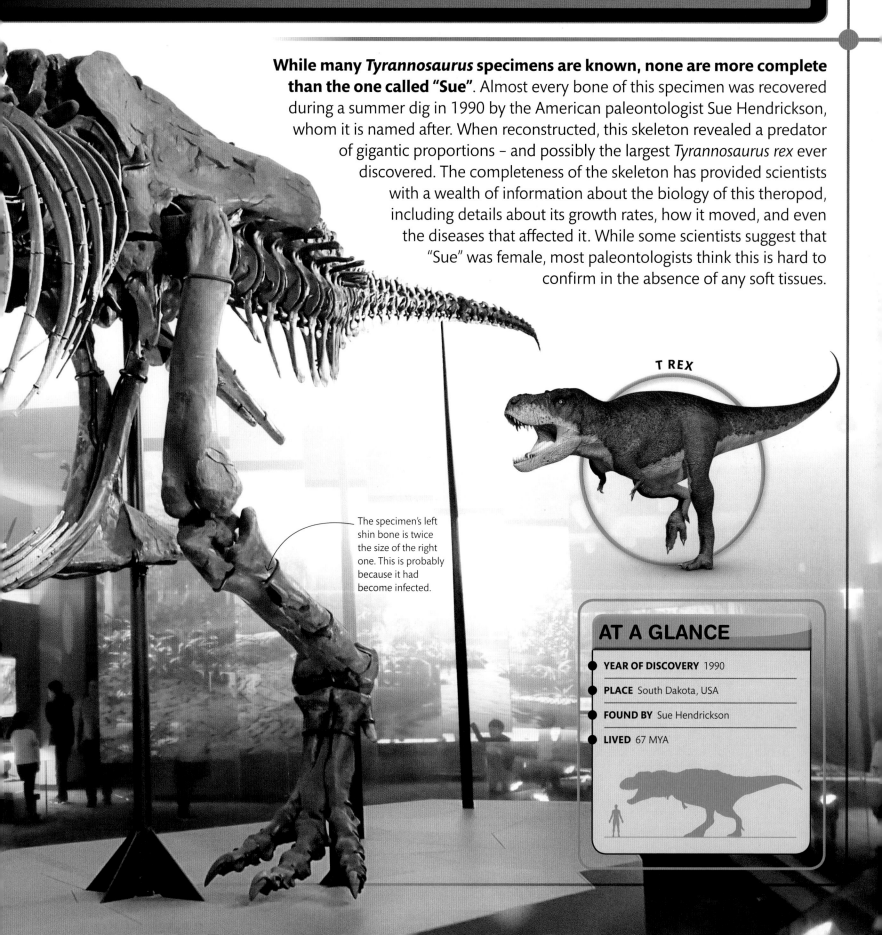

FAMOUS FOSSIL
SUE, THE T REX

While many *Tyrannosaurus* specimens are known, none are more complete than the one called "Sue". Almost every bone of this specimen was recovered during a summer dig in 1990 by the American paleontologist Sue Hendrickson, whom it is named after. When reconstructed, this skeleton revealed a predator of gigantic proportions – and possibly the largest *Tyrannosaurus rex* ever discovered. The completeness of the skeleton has provided scientists with a wealth of information about the biology of this theropod, including details about its growth rates, how it moved, and even the diseases that affected it. While some scientists suggest that "Sue" was female, most paleontologists think this is hard to confirm in the absence of any soft tissues.

T REX

The specimen's left shin bone is twice the size of the right one. This is probably because it had become infected.

AT A GLANCE

YEAR OF DISCOVERY 1990

PLACE South Dakota, USA

FOUND BY Sue Hendrickson

LIVED 67 MYA

FOSSIL WALL

What appears here to be a wall of bones is really a tilted bed of sandstone rock containing the scattered fossils of the dinosaurs *Allosaurus*, *Apatosaurus*, *Camarasaurus*, *Diplodocus*, and *Stegosaurus*. It is located in the Dinosaur National Monument, in Utah, USA, where paleontologists have found a jumble of dinosaur fossils. These dinosaurs all died near an ancient river and their bones were mixed up and deposited onto a sandbar.

ILL-FATED BUNCH
PSITTACOSAURUS YOUNG

Paleontologists were initially puzzled when they discovered this group of 30 young *Psittacosaurus* fossilized together alongside the skull of a larger individual. Many experts wondered how these dinosaurs came to be in one place, with some suggesting that it was evidence of a parent taking care of its young. However, further examination revealed that although the larger individual was older than the others, it was not yet an adult. Paleontologists now think that this set of fossils shows cooperation among *Psittacosaurus* young of various ages, probably as a way of defending themselves against predators.

The skull size suggests that the larger individual was probably around four or five years old.

AT A GLANCE

- **YEAR OF DISCOVERY** 2012
- **PLACE** Liaoning, China
- **STUDIED BY** Brandon Hedrick and team
- **LIVED** 125–120 MYA

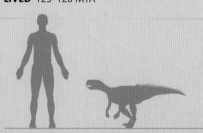

VOLCANIC MUDFLOW

After a volcanic eruption, ash-laden debris often gets mixed with water to form devastating mudflows, which can cover vast areas in concrete-like mud. The group of *Psittacosaurus* young shown in the main image may have been the victims of such a mudflow. They were found preserved in volcanic rock, and the orientation of their bodies suggested that they had been engulfed together.

NOT A NEST

Although these fossils look like they are embedded in a nest, on closer inspection it is clear that this is not the case. Nests made by animals on land have a depression and a ridge around the outside, which this specimen lacks.

STUNNING SCIENCE

171

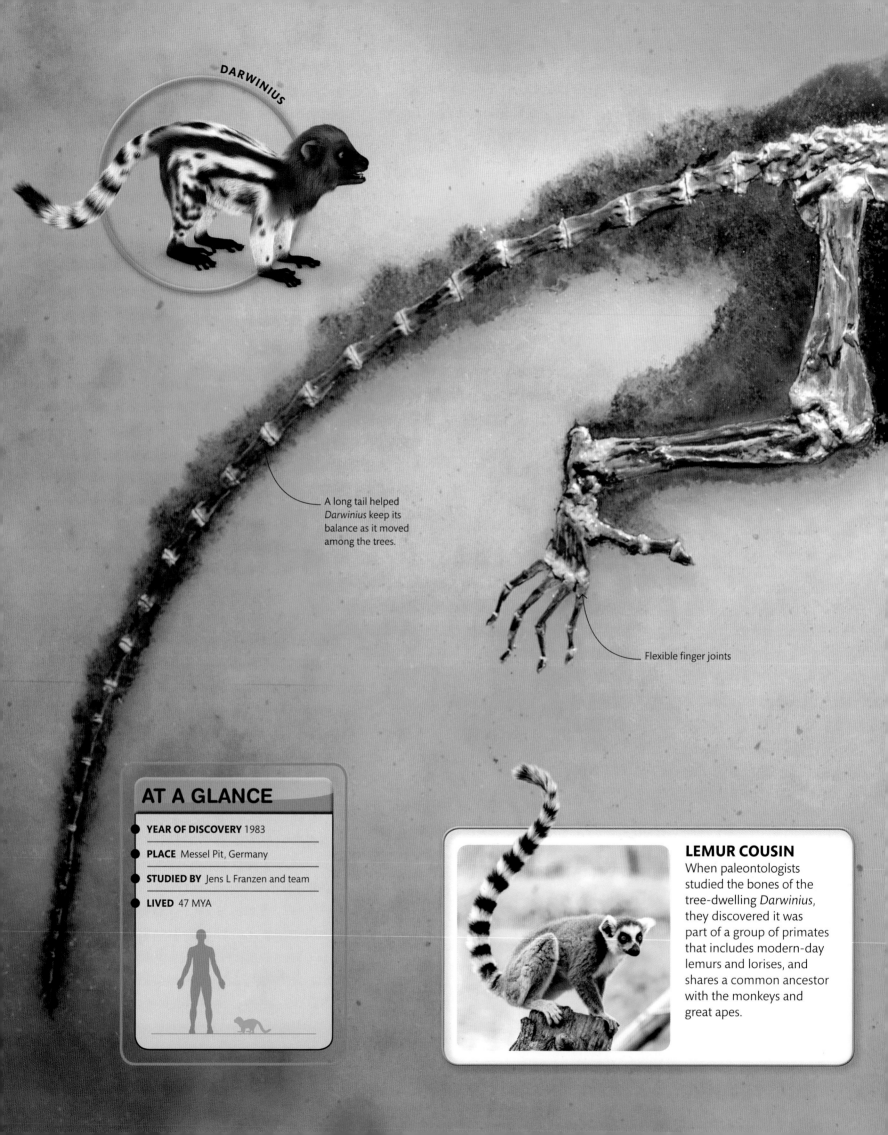

DARWINIUS

A long tail helped
Darwinius keep its
balance as it moved
among the trees.

Flexible finger joints

AT A GLANCE

- **YEAR OF DISCOVERY** 1983

- **PLACE** Messel Pit, Germany

- **STUDIED BY** Jens L Franzen and team

- **LIVED** 47 MYA

LEMUR COUSIN

When paleontologists
studied the bones of the
tree-dwelling *Darwinius*,
they discovered it was
part of a group of primates
that includes modern-day
lemurs and lorises, and
shares a common ancestor
with the monkeys and
great apes.

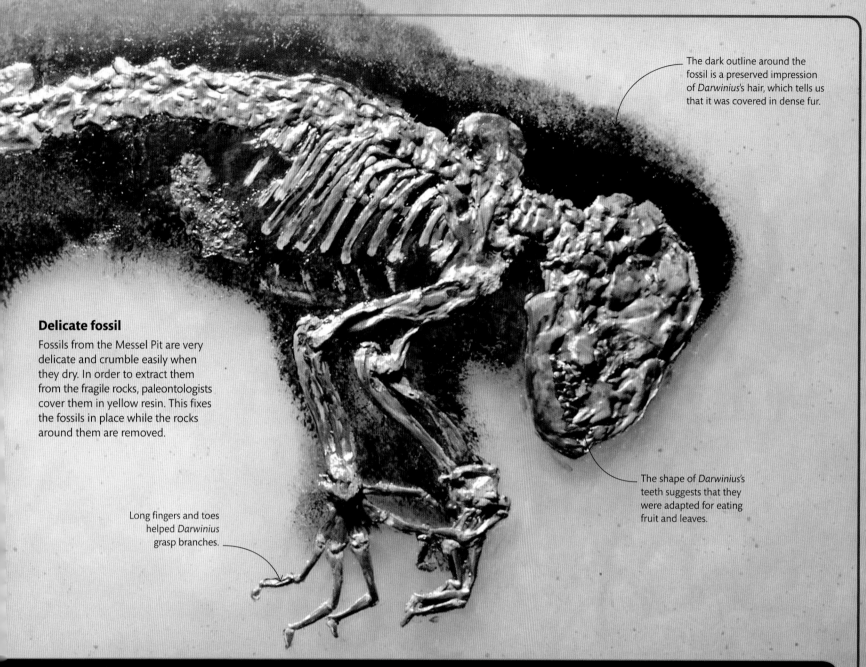

The dark outline around the fossil is a preserved impression of *Darwinius*'s hair, which tells us that it was covered in dense fur.

Delicate fossil

Fossils from the Messel Pit are very delicate and crumble easily when they dry. In order to extract them from the fragile rocks, paleontologists cover them in yellow resin. This fixes the fossils in place while the rocks around them are removed.

The shape of *Darwinius*'s teeth suggests that they were adapted for eating fruit and leaves.

Long fingers and toes helped *Darwinius* grasp branches.

PERFECTLY PRESERVED

DARWINIUS

Nicknamed "Ida", this remarkable fossil of an early primate called *Darwinius* caused quite a stir when it was first purchased from a private collector and studied. Originally hailed as the "missing link" in the evolution of humans from monkeys, paleontologists have since questioned this fossil's importance in understanding our own origins. Today, *Darwinius* is considered to be only distantly related to human ancestors. This specimen was found in an area in Germany called the Messel Pit that is famous for its exceptional fossils, including some that still have evidence of soft tissues such as fur. Millions of years ago, the Messel Pit used to be a deep lake that was poor in oxygen. Any animal that fell in sank to the bottom, where it was covered in soft mud, and decomposed very slowly. This preserved its features as it turned into a fossil.

PETRIFIED ARMOUR
BOREALOPELTA

Hidden within a large block of stone and accidentally discovered by miners, this fossil is one of the best examples of excellently preserved dinosaur skin. The block was found in a marine deposit, which formed in a prehistoric ocean. The paleontologists from the Royal Tyrrell Museum in Canada who went to examine the fossil thought they would be looking at another of the marine reptiles that are common in those deposits. Little did they know that within the hard rock lay a large armoured dinosaur, later named *Borealopelta*. It was a herbivore that belonged to a family of heavily armoured ankylosaurs, and may have grown up to 5.5 m (18 ft) in length. The fossil was in such a good condition that scientists have even been able to reconstruct *Borealopelta's* reddish colour.

BOREALOPELTA

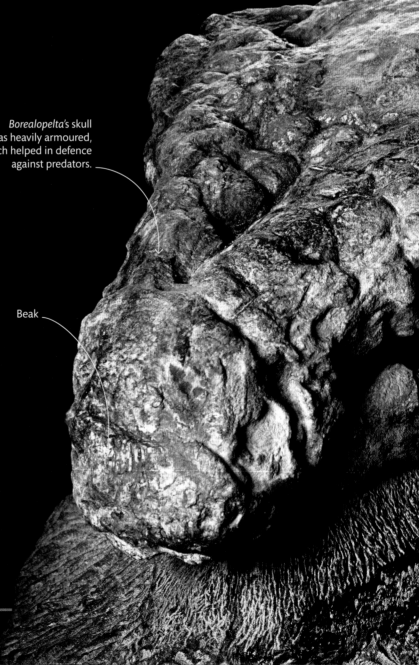
Borealopelta's skull was heavily armoured, which helped in defence against predators.

Beak

FOSSILIZED COLOURS
The preserved pigments in the fossil suggest that *Borealopelta* had a rusty red back and a lightly coloured belly. This camouflaged it in its plant-rich coastal habitat. At this time predators were so deadly that even large armoured dinosaurs needed to try to hide.

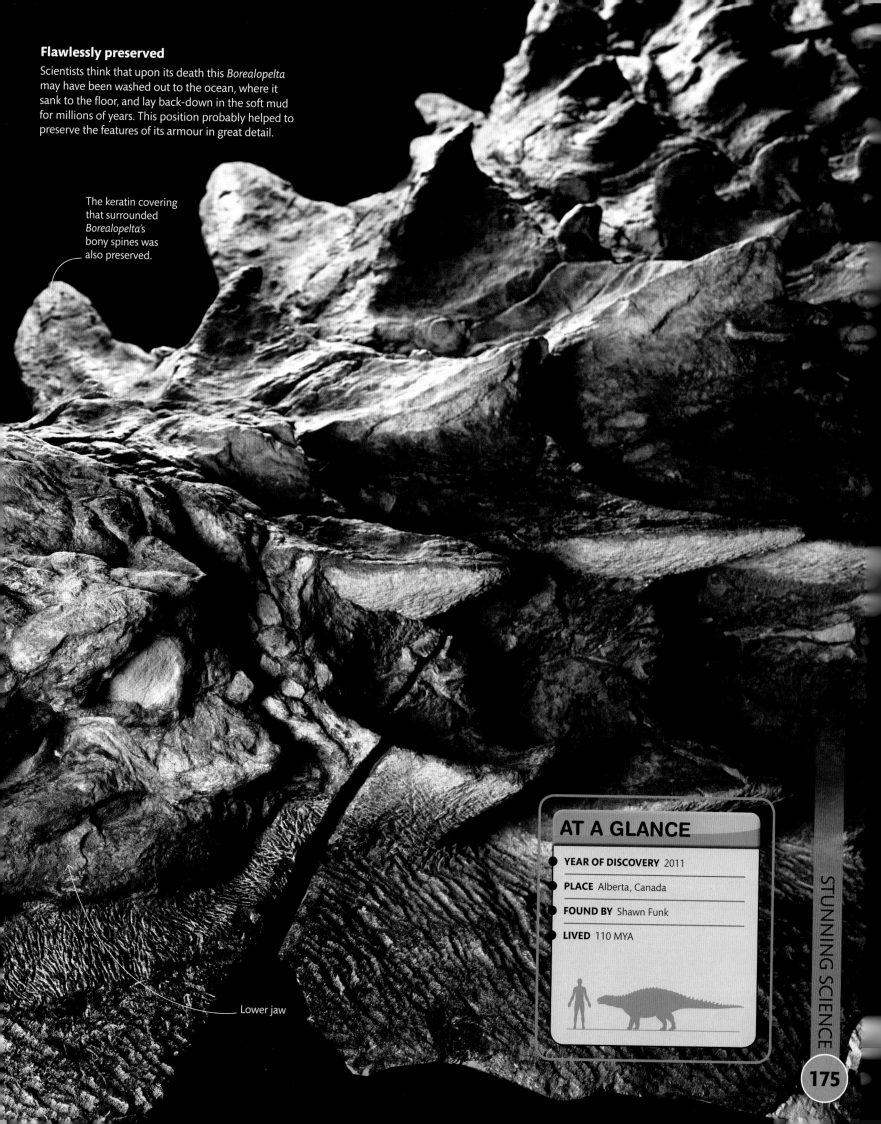

Flawlessly preserved

Scientists think that upon its death this *Borealopelta* may have been washed out to the ocean, where it sank to the floor, and lay back-down in the soft mud for millions of years. This position probably helped to preserve the features of its armour in great detail.

The keratin covering that surrounded *Borealopelta*'s bony spines was also preserved.

Lower jaw

AT A GLANCE

YEAR OF DISCOVERY 2011

PLACE Alberta, Canada

FOUND BY Shawn Funk

LIVED 110 MYA

TRAPPED IN AMBER
BIRD HATCHLING

Small animals can get caught in the golden-yellow, sticky resin that oozes out of the bark of certain trees. As the resin fossilizes into amber, it creates a seal, preserving delicate soft tissue such as the skin and muscles of creatures trapped inside, in exquisite detail. This means that amber fossils offer some of the clearest insights into the prehistoric world. One such glimpse comes from this fossil, which contains the hatchling of an extinct bird, known as an enantiornithine. Trapped in the fossil's resin prison, parts of the bird's skull, feet, and wings can be seen in extraordinary detail. Hundreds of different species of ancient creatures, including birds and insects, and even portions of dinosaur tails, have been found preserved in amber.

Tiny, clawed wings can just about be seen with the naked eye.

EARLY BIRDS
The enantiornithines were a group of birds capable of powered flight. Their fossils show that they had toothed beaks and wing claws. These tiny birds became extinct at the end of the Cretaceous Period along with the pterosaurs, marine reptiles, and most dinosaurs.

Preserved impression of feather

AT A GLANCE

- **YEAR OF DISCOVERY** 2017
- **PLACE** Myanmar
- **STUDIED BY** Lida Xing and colleagues
- **LIVED** 99 MYA

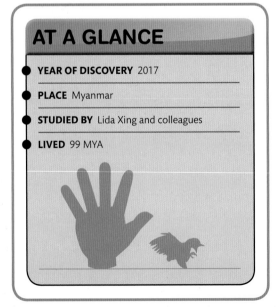

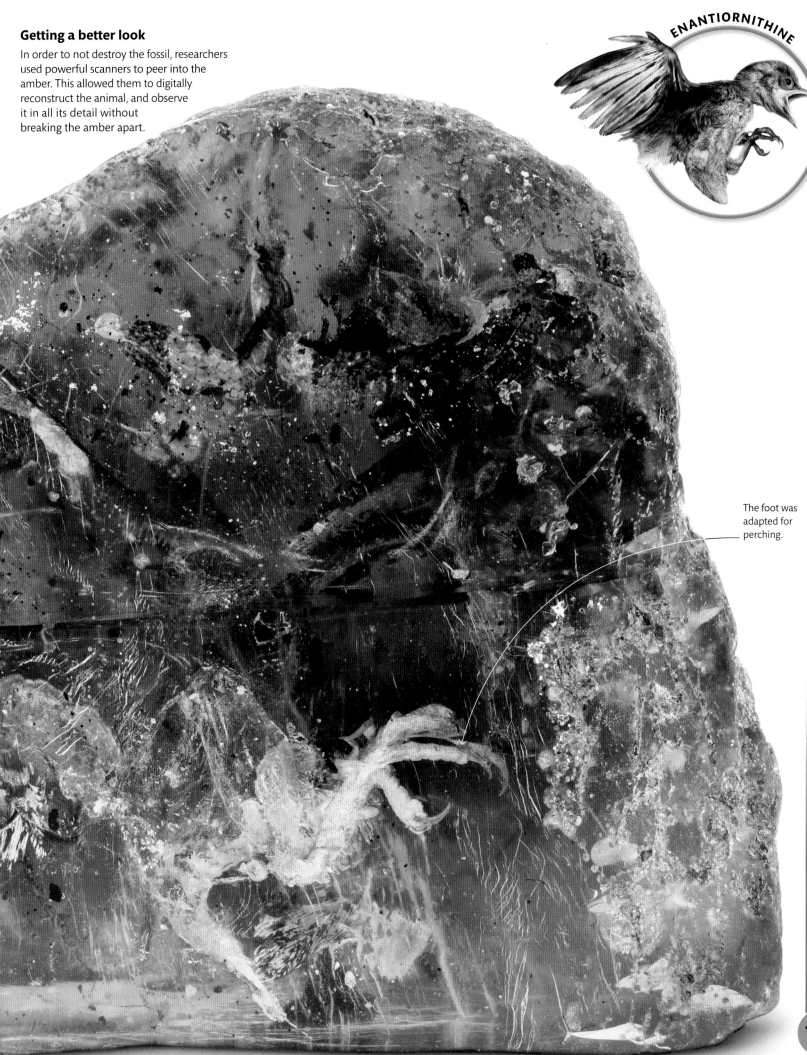

Getting a better look

In order to not destroy the fossil, researchers used powerful scanners to peer into the amber. This allowed them to digitally reconstruct the animal, and observe it in all its detail without breaking the amber apart.

ENANTIORNITHINE

The foot was adapted for perching.

PRESERVED IN AMBER

Around 130 million years ago, this fly buzzed around tropical forests in what is now Lebanon. As it landed on a tree, it was caught in resin, which fossilized over time into amber. Lebanese amber is famous as a rich source of insect remains, and many ancient relatives of modern insects have been found trapped inside these golden nuggets.

Paleontologists are now able to peer inside the fossilized bones of prehistoric creatures thanks to powerful new technologies. Using CT scanners, scientists can digitally create three-dimensional (3D) models of dinosaur skulls. Examining these models provides scientists with a wealth of information about the dinosaur's soft tissues, and studies of these models can tell us a great deal about the creature's biology. This model shows the skull of the theropod *Majungasaurus*, and reveals that the skulls of many theropods had lots of air-filled pockets, called sinuses. Some of the coloured patches in this model show the sinuses – these probably made the creature's skull lighter and may also have helped it control its body temperature.

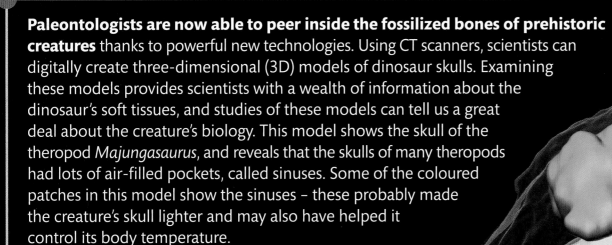

The yellow portion shown here is *Majungasaurus's* airway, which is connected to its nostrils at the front.

AT A GLANCE

- **YEAR OF DISCOVERY** 1896

- **PLACE** Madagascar

- **STUDIED BY** Larry Witmer and Ryan Ridgely

- **LIVED** 69–66 MYA

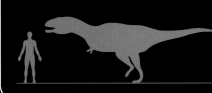

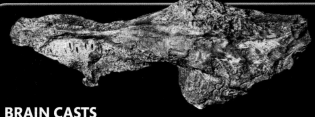
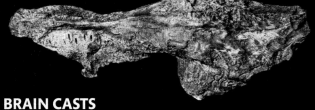

BRAIN CASTS
Before the development of powerful scanners, researchers used casts to study the brains of prehistoric creatures. These casts are sometimes made from hardened sediment that filled a skull during fossilization, such as the *Tyrannosaurus* brain cast seen here. Scientists have also made artificial skull casts using plaster, but this process can damage delicate fossils and so it cannot be used on rare specimens.

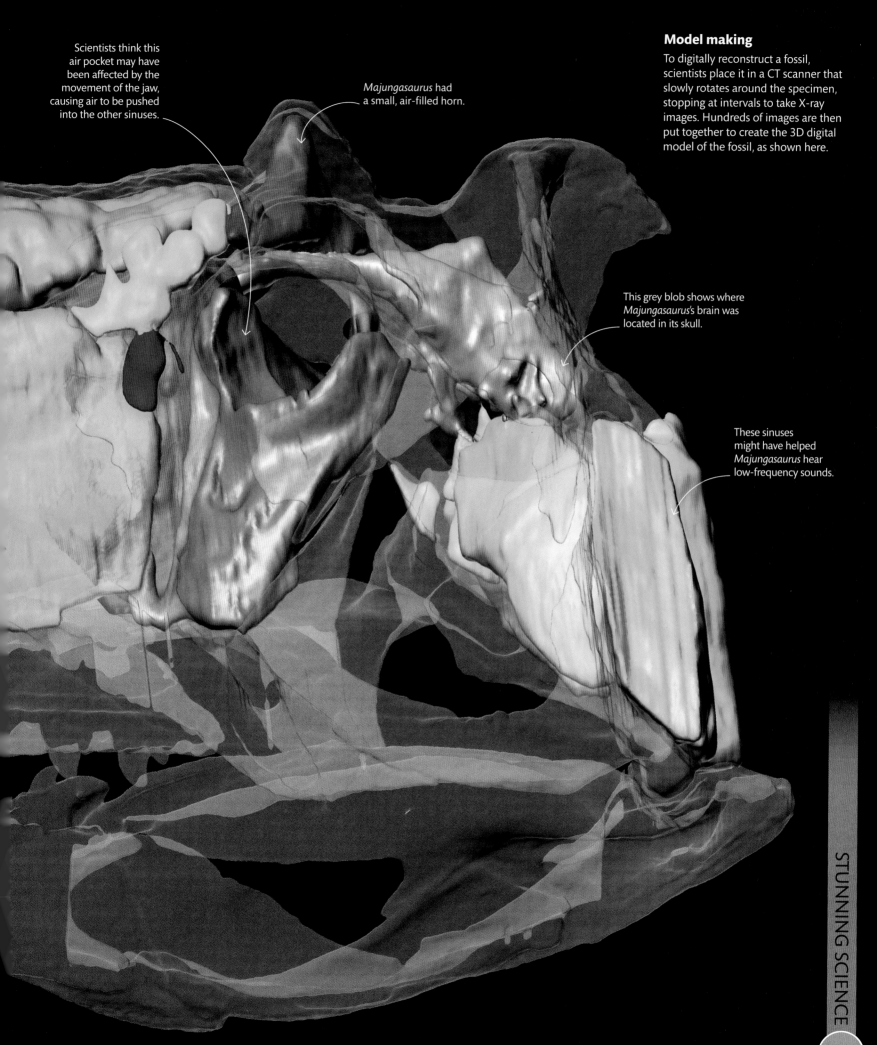

Scientists think this air pocket may have been affected by the movement of the jaw, causing air to be pushed into the other sinuses.

Majungasaurus had a small, air-filled horn.

Model making

To digitally reconstruct a fossil, scientists place it in a CT scanner that slowly rotates around the specimen, stopping at intervals to take X-ray images. Hundreds of images are then put together to create the 3D digital model of the fossil, as shown here.

This grey blob shows where *Majungasaurus*'s brain was located in its skull.

These sinuses might have helped *Majungasaurus* hear low-frequency sounds.

PREHISTORIC POO
COPROLITES

Shark coprolite

Fossilized dung might be one of the last places you would expect to find clues about the lifestyles and habits of prehistoric creatures. However, coprolites (the scientific term for fossilized animal droppings) are a gold mine of valuable information and provide some of the best evidence of what these different animals ate. Coprolites also reveal what kinds of plant grew in the distant past, and the types of gut parasite and microorganism that lived inside the digestive systems of dinosaurs and other prehistoric animals.

This coprolite was found in a fossil-rich region called the Morrison Formation in Utah, USA.

The shape and surface pattern of a rock that looks like a coprolite can be matched with dung from modern animals in order to confirm its identity.

MARY ANNING

The famous British fossil hunter Mary Anning was the first person to examine fossilized dung. In 1824, she found odd-looking "stones" full of fish bones among the fossils of an ichthyosaur on the south coast of England, and shared her finds with paleontologist William Buckland. Together they concluded that this meant ichthyosaurs hunted small fish.

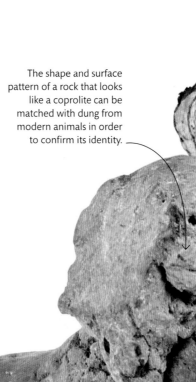

The **largest** known **coprolite** is 30 cm (12 in) long, and is thought to have belonged to a *T rex*.

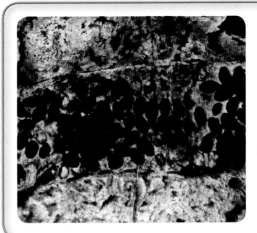

LOOKING INSIDE

Paleontologists are able to get more information about coprolites using microscopes and scanners. This image shows a microscopic view of a shark coprolite from the Paleozoic Era. The presence of unhatched tapeworm eggs shows that this parasite was present in the creature's intestines.

Coprolite clues

Paleontologists need evidence to identify coprolites. Fossilized dung of ancient aquatic predators often contains fish bones, while the plant pollen in some poo helps experts date the specimens. Fragments of bone and muscle found in the prehistoric dung of some theropods suggest that food passed quickly through their digestive system. However, determining which prehistoric creature a coprolite belonged to is a harder task.

Fossilized dung is difficult to find because it often rapidly breaks down and can look like a normal rock.

Fossil sites

To find dinosaur fossils you need to look for the right rocks. Paleozoic or Cenozoic rock layers at Earth's surface come from the wrong time period. Some of the best deposits tend to be those laid down by rivers and lakes during the Mesozoic Era.

Tyrannosaurus

Tyrannosaurus fossils have been found in the Hell Creek Formation.

DINOSAUR NATIONAL MONUMENT, USA

HELL CREEK FORMATION, USA

ISCHIGUALASTO FORMATION, ARGENTINA

Eoraptor

NORTH AMERICA

Some of the best fossil sites in the world are found in North America. In fact, some deposits are so full of fossils that it's impossible to collect them all. One such location, in the state of Colorado, has been named the Dinosaur National Monument because of the large number of fossils found among its formations.

SOUTH AMERICA

With a large part of the continent covered by the dense Amazon rainforest, it has been difficult for paleontologists to access likely fossil sites in South America. Even so, several important areas have been discovered, such as the Ischigualasto Formation, which revealed fossils of *Herrerasaurus* and *Eoraptor*, some of the earliest dinosaurs ever to exist.

FOSSIL FINDS

Fossils of prehistoric creatures have been found on all seven continents, though some areas are more dinosaur-rich than others. There are many reasons for this variation in the number of fossils found – everything from inaccessible terrain to the number of people out looking for fossils. However, as paleontology becomes more global, and scientific methods develop, fossil finds are becoming increasingly common across the world.

EUROPE

Our knowledge of prehistoric creatures began in Europe in the early 1800s when the very first dinosaurs to be named were discovered in the UK. There are fossil-rich sites across the continent, such as Solnhofen in Germany, where the winged *Archaeopteryx* was found.

Archaeopteryx

ASIA

This continent is home to some remarkable fossils, many of which can be found within its unique rock formations, as seen in the Gobi Desert. In China, amber specimens have preserved the soft tissues of some dinosaurs and prehistoric animals.

Protoceratops

Fossils of this small herbivore are common in the rocks of Mongolia.

AUSTRALIA

Fossils of prehistoric animals from Australia are rare. Dinosaur fossils were first discovered there in 1903, at a site now known as Dinosaur Cove. Recent finds include one spectacular set of bones, which have a blue colour because they were fossilized in opal.

A well-preserved pliosaur fossil was discovered in Queensland in 1990.

Pliosaur

AFRICA

The vast deserts and steamy rainforests of Africa make this continent a tricky place to go looking for fossils. However, in recent years many areas, such as the fossil deposits in the Ténéré Desert, have been found to be rich in ancient life, and fascinating finds have become increasingly common.

ANTARCTICA

A harsh climate and vast inaccessible areas make Antarctica one of the most hostile places on Earth. However, this region was covered in lush forests during the Jurassic Period and would have teemed with life. Paleontologists need special equipment to reach fossil sites and have only found a few specimens among the hard rocks so far.

Mt Kirkpatrick, Antarctica

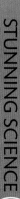

GLOSSARY

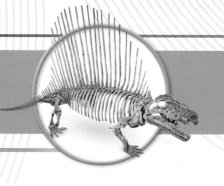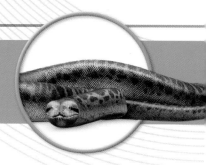

ABELISAURID
A type of large, meat-eating theropod. Abelisaurids thrived during the Cretaceous Period.

ADAPTATION
A special feature of an organism that makes it better suited to its environment.

AIR SAC
A little growth of tissue filled with air. Air sacs help a creature breathe and keep its body light.

AMBER
Sticky tree resin that has become hard and tough over many millions of years.

AMBUSH
A surprise attack by a predator on an unsuspecting prey.

AMMONITE
A marine mollusc with a coiled shell and octopus-like tentacles that was common in the Mesozoic Era.

ANATOMY
A branch of science involving the study of the physical structure and internal workings of all living things.

ANKYLOSAUR
A type of ornithischian (bird-hipped) dinosaur. Ankylosaurs were armoured plant-eaters with a body covered in bony plates.

ARCHOSAUR
One of a group of reptiles that includes the dinosaurs, pterosaurs, and the extinct relatives of crocodiles and alligators, as well as modern-day birds and crocodylians.

ARTHROPOD
An invertebrate with a segmented body and a hard outer covering called an exoskeleton. Living examples of arthropods include insects and spiders.

ASTEROID
A large rocky object that orbits the Sun. Asteroids are bigger than meteors but smaller than dwarf planets.

BONE BED
A massive deposit of fossil bones.

BROODING
Adult animals keeping eggs or hatchlings warm by covering them with their feathered bodies or wings.

CARBONIFEROUS
The fifth period of the Paleozoic Era. It began 358 million years ago and ended 298 million years ago.

CENOZOIC
The era that followed the Mesozoic. It started 66 million years ago and continues in the present day.

CERATOPSIAN
A type of ornithischian (bird-hipped) dinosaur. Ceratopsians were plant-eaters with horns on the head or bony frills around the skull.

COPROLITE
Fossilized animal droppings, which often contain fragments of undigested food.

CRETACEOUS
The third period of the Mesozoic Era. It began 145 million years ago and ended 66 million years ago.

CROCODYLIAN
A group of reptiles that includes modern-day crocodiles and alligators as well as extinct relatives, such as *Deinosuchus*.

CT SCANNER
A machine that takes detailed pictures of the insides of a creature's body or of its parts.

DENTAL BATTERY
An arrangement of small, interlocking teeth in some plant-eating dinosaurs that help grind up tough plant matter.

DICRAEOSAURID
A type of small, short-necked sauropod. Dicraeosaurids lived in the span of time between the Early Jurassic and Cretaceous periods.

DIGITS
The fingers or toes of limbed vertebrates.

DISPLAY
In animals, a demonstration of fitness or strength, usually to frighten off a rival or to attract a mate.

ECOSYSTEM
A community or collection of living organisms that interact with each other and with their surrounding environment in a particular way.

ENAMEL
The hard outer layer on the teeth of most animals that makes the teeth resistant to wear and tear.

ERA
A span of geological time that defines a phase of the history of life, such as the Paleozoic or Mesozoic. Each era is made up of periods.

EUKARYOTE
An organism made out of a complex cell or cells containing nuclei and other structures that are enclosed in membranes. All animals, plants and fungi are eukaryotes.

FILTER FEEDER
An animal that feeds by straining shrimp, algae, or other small organisms out of the water.

FRILL
A bony, platelike extension around the neck of certain animals.

HABITAT
The natural home environment of an animal or plant.

HADROSAUR
A type of ornithopod with a complex set of teeth, called a dental battery, and a duck-like beak.

HATCHLING
A newly hatched baby animal.

HETERODONT
An animal with two or more differently shaped sets of teeth in its jaws, such as sharp teeth for biting and cheek teeth for chewing food.

ICHTHYOSAUR
A type of dolphin-like marine reptile that was common for much of the Mesozoic Era.

INCUBATE
To keep eggs warm so they develop and hatch.

IRIDIUM
A type of chemical element that is more abundant in asteroids, meteors, and other space rocks than on Earth.

KERATIN
A tough substance found in the hair, feathers, scales, claws, and horns of most animals.

LARVA
The young form of an insect, which looks different from its parents, and often eats different food.

LIGAMENTS
Strong, slightly elastic, cordlike structures in an animal's body that attach bones to each other.

MAMMAL
One of a group of warm-blooded, often hairy vertebrates that feed their young on milk supplied by the mother.

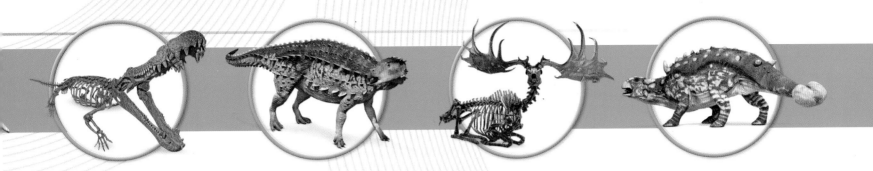

MANIRAPTORAN
A type of long-armed theropod, such as *Velociraptor*.

MARSUPIAL
A mammal that gives birth to very small live young and rears them in a pouch.

MESOZOIC
The era that followed the Paleozoic. It began 240 million years ago and ended 66 million years ago, and includes the Triassic, Jurassic, and Cretaceous periods.

NON-BIRD DINOSAUR
As modern birds are surviving dinosaurs, palaeontologists use this term to describe dinosaurs that fall outside the bird group in the family tree. These dinosaurs died out at the end of the Cretaceous.

ORNITHISCHIAN
A member of one of the two major dinosaur groups. It is also known as a "bird-hipped" dinosaur.

ORNITHOMIMID
A type of fast-running theropod with a long neck and slender legs, similar in appearance to a modern-day ostrich.

ORNITHOPOD
A type of ornithischian (bird-hipped) dinosaur. Ornithopods were plant-eaters with birdlike feet. Examples of ornithopods include the hadrosaurs.

OSTEODERM
A bony plate embedded in the skin. Rows of osteoderms made up the armour of some dinosaurs, and are seen in some modern animals such as crocodiles and alligators as well.

PACHYCEPHALOSAUR
A type of ornithischian (bird-hipped) dinosaur. Pachycephalosaurs were plant-eaters with a thick, bony dome on the skull.

PALEONTOLOGIST
A scientist who studies fossils and other evidence of prehistoric life.

PALEONTOLOGY
The study of fossils and prehistoric life.

PALEOZOIC
The era that came before the Mesozoic. It began 541 million years ago and ended 252 million years ago.

PEDIPALPS
A pair of tiny front limbs found in some arthropods, such as spiders and scorpions.

PLESIOSAUR
A type of marine reptile with four long flippers. Some plesiosaurs had very long necks.

PRIMATE
One of a group of mammals that includes lemurs, monkeys, apes, and humans.

PROKARYOTE
Any single-celled organism, such as a bacterium, with a cell that has a simple structure and lacks a well-defined nucleus.

PTEROSAUR
A type of flying reptile that lived during the Mesozoic Era. Its wings were made of stretched skin supported by the bones of an elongated finger in each forelimb.

SAURISCHIAN
A member of one of the two major dinosaur groups. It is also known as a "lizard-hipped" dinosaur.

SAUROPOD
A type of saurischian (lizard-hipped) dinosaur. Sauropods were plant-eaters that walked on all fours and had a long neck.

SCAVENGER
An animal that lives on the remains of dead creatures and scraps left behind by other animals.

SCUTE
A tough, often protective plate embedded in the skin. It has a bony base and a covering of scaly keratin.

SERRATED
A surface that is saw-toothed, like the edge of a bread knife.

SINUS
An air-filled cavity in the skull.

SPECIES
A particular type of living thing that can breed with others of its type.

STEGOSAUR
A type of ornithischian (bird-hipped) dinosaur. Stegosaurs were armoured plant-eaters with large plates along their back.

SYNAPSID
One of a group of vertebrates that includes mammals and their ancestors.

THEROPOD
A type of saurischian (lizard-hipped) dinosaur. Theropods were often meat-eaters and bipedal. Some theropods gave rise to birds.

THYREOPHORAN
One of a group of dinosaurs that includes the armoured ankylosaurs and stegosaurs.

TRACKWAY
A trail of fossilized footprints.

TROODONTID
A type of small, agile theropod.

TYRANNOSAURID
A type of large, meat-eating theropod such as *Tyrannosaurus*. Tyrannosaurids evolved in

the Late Cretaceous, and had huge jaws adapted for bone-crunching bites.

ULTRAVIOLET (UV)
Electromagnetic radiation with wavelengths shorter than visible light but longer than X-rays.

VERTEBRAE
The bones forming the backbone of a vertebrate animal.

VERTEBRATE
An animal with an internal skeleton and a backbone made up of vertebrae. Dinosaurs, mammals, birds, and fish are all vertebrates.

WINGSPAN
The measurement from the tip of one wing of an animal to the tip of the other when the wings are outstretched.

ZOOPLANKTON
A tiny animal that lives in the ocean. Some zooplankton spend their whole lives floating around.

Abbreviations used in this book	
/	per – for example, km/h means kilometre per hour
cm	centimetre
°C	degrees Celsius
°F	degrees Fahrenheit
ft	foot
g	gram
in	inch
kg	kilogram
km	kilometre
lb	pound
m	metre
mph	miles per hour
MYA	million years ago
oz	ounce

INDEX

ACKNOWLEDGMENTS

The publisher would like to thank the following people for their help with making the book: Virien Chopra, Ashwin Khurana, and Sukriti Kapoor for editorial assistance; Stefan Podhorodecki and Sanya Jain for design assistance; Peter Bull for illustration assistance; Steve Crozier for retouching; Ashok Kumar, Vijay Kandwal, and Vikram Singh for assistance with colour work; Priyanka Sharma, Harish Aggarwal, and Saloni Singh for the jacket; Victoria Pyke for proofreading; and Elizabeth Wise for the Index.

Picture Credits

The publisher would like to thank the following for their kind permission to reproduce their photographs:

(Key: a-above; b-below/bottom; c-centre; f-far; l-left; r-right; t-top)

6-7 Great Plains Dinosaur Museum & Field Station. **6 Alamy Stock Photo:** The Natural History Museum (clb). **7 Getty Images:** Bart Maat / Contributor / AFP (tc). **iStockphoto.com:** Benedek / E+ (tr). **Science Photo Library:** Philippe Psaila (cra, crb). **8 Dreamstime.com:** 7xpert (cr). **10-11 Getty Images:** Leonello Calvetti / Stocktrek Images. **10 Science Photo Library:** Chris Hellier (cra); Millard H. Sharp (clb). **11 Alamy Stock Photo:** Zoonar GmbH / Christian Wei (bc). **James Kuether:** (br). **12 Dorling Kindersley:** James Kuether (clb). **13 Dorling Kindersley:** James Kuether (crb). **15 123RF.com:** Sayompu Chamnankit (tc/ Footprints); Albertus Engbers (tc). **Alamy Stock Photo:** Jack Barr (tr). **Dorling Kindersley:** Natural History Museum (ftr). **22-23 Science Photo Library:** Walter Myers. **24-25 Alamy Stock Photo:** Universal Images Group North America LLC / DeAgostini. **26-27 Science Photo Library:** Millard H. Sharp / Science Source. **27 James Kuether:** (tc). **36-37 Pierre Jayet**. **40-41 Science Photo Library:** John Sibbick. **42-43 Science Photo Library:** Jaime Chirinos. **45 iStockphoto.com:** Breckeni (cr). **46-47 Damir G Martin**. **52 © Nikolay Zverkov:** (clb). **59 Jürgen Christian Harf | www.pterosaurier.de:** (br). **60-61 Wikipedia:** Gadfium | CC0 1.0. **63 Alamy Stock Photo:** Xinhua (tl). **65 Getty Images:** Dean Mouhtaropoulos / Staff / Getty Images Europe (cl). **70-71 James Kuether**. **80-81 James Kuether**. **83 Getty Images:** Kevork Djansezian / Staff / Getty Images North America (tl). **90 Alamy Stock Photo:** Gaertner (clb). **95 Dorling Kindersley:** Natural History Museum, London (tr). **96-97 James Kuether**. **99 Alamy Stock Photo:** Dmitry Rukhlenko - Travel Photos (cr). **Lineart by Robinson Kunz (teratophoneus. deviantart.com/) | Colour by Rebecca Slater (www.artstation. com/r-slater):** (cr/Titanoceratops). **102 Dorling Kindersley:** Senckenberg Gesellschaft Fuer Naturforschugn (cla). **106-107 James Kuether. 114-115 Rocky Mountain Dinosaur Resource Center. 114 Nobumichi Tamura:** (tc). **116-117 Science Photo Library:** Millard H. Sharp / Science Source. **120-121 Damir G Martin**. **125 Florida Museum of Natural History:** Photo by Kristen Grace (tc). **129 Mary Evans Picture Library:** Natural History Museum (cra). **133 Dreamstime.com:** S100apm (cb). **134 Roman Uchytel:** (cr). **136-137 Getty Images:** AFP / Stringer. **138-139 Smithsonian Institution, Washington, DC. 139 Science Photo Library:** Roman Uchytel (tc). **142 Science Photo Library:** UCL, Grant Museum Of Zoology (c). **146-147 Dreamstime.com:** Solarseven. **147 Alamy Stock Photo:** Dinodia Photos (tc). **148-149 Science Photo Library:** Chris Hellier. **148 Nat Geo Image Collection:** Robert Clark (bl). **150 Photo: Helmut Tischlinger:** (bc). **150-151 Alamy Stock Photo:** Steve Vidler. **151 Dorling Kindersley:** James Kuether (tr). **152-153 Alamy Stock Photo:** Kevin Schafer. **153 Getty Images:** Bettmann (crb). **154-155 Louie Psihoyos ©psihoyos.com**. **155 Dorling Kindersley:** James Kuether (tc). **156-157 Alamy Stock Photo:** The Natural History Museum. **158-159 Photo: Helmut Tischlinger**. **158 James Kuether:** (tl). **Photo: Helmut Tischlinger:** (bc). **Nobumichi Tamura:** (bl). **160-161 Louie Psihoyos ©psihoyos.com**. **161 Alamy Stock Photo:** Henry Beeker (cra). **162-163 Dorling Kindersley:** Natural History Museum. **164-165 naturepl.com:** Pete Oxford. **165 Alamy Stock Photo:** Lee Foster (tl). **166 Getty Images:** Field Museum Library / Contributor / Premium Archive (clb). **166-167 Shutterstock:** ChicagoPhotographer. **167 Dorling Kindersley:** James Kuether (cr). **168-169 Ardea:** Francois Gohier. **170 Alamy Stock Photo:** Science History Images (bc). **170-171 Rex by Shutterstock:** Jinyuan Liu. **172-173 Alamy Stock Photo:** Martin Shields. **172 Dreamstime.com:** Kajornyot (bc). **174-175 Nat Geo Image Collection:** Robert Clark. **174 Alamy Stock Photo:** Robert Clark / National Geographic Image Collection (bl). **Science Photo Library:** Masato Hattori (clb). **176 Shutterstock:** Akkharat Jarusilawong (cl). **176-177 Dr Lida XING. 177 Dr Lida XING:** (tr). **178-179 Getty Images:** Marc Deville / Contributor / Gamma-Rapho. **180-181 Courtesy of WitmerLab at Ohio University / Lawrence M. Witmer, PhD. 180 Science Photo Library:** Millard H. Sharp (clb). **182 Alamy Stock Photo:** The Natural History Museum (cl); RGB Ventures / SuperStock / Fred Hirschmann (cr). **Dorling Kindersley:** Courtesy of Dorset Dinosaur Museum (cla). **iStockphoto.com:** Gfrandsen (bc). **182-183 123RF.com:** Alexeykonovalenko. **183 PLoS Biology:** Dentzien-Dias PC, Poinar G Jr, de Figueiredo AEQ, Pacheco ACL, Horn BLD, Schultz CL (2013) Tapeworm Eggs in a 270 Million-Year-Old Shark Coprolite. PLoS ONE 8(1): e55007. https://doi. org/10.1371/journal.pone.0055007 (tc). **184 Alamy Stock Photo:** Chuck Haney / Danita Delimont (cra); Prisma by Dukas Presseagentur GmbH / Newman Mark (cla); Florian Neukirchen (c). **185 Alamy Stock Photo:** Filmfoto-03edit (tl); Miguel Galmés (tr); Imagebroker / White Star / Monica Gumm (cr); Kim Westerskov (br). **Getty Images:** Maurice Ascani / Contributor / Gamma-Rapho (clb). **186 Science Photo Library:** Millard H. Sharp / Science Source (tc). **187 Science Photo Library:** Millard H. Sharp / Science Source (tl). **Smithsonian Institution, Washington, DC:** (tc). **188 Alamy Stock Photo:** Kevin Schafer (tr). **Science Photo Library:** John Sibbick (tc)

All other images © Dorling Kindersley

For further information see: **www.dkimages.com**

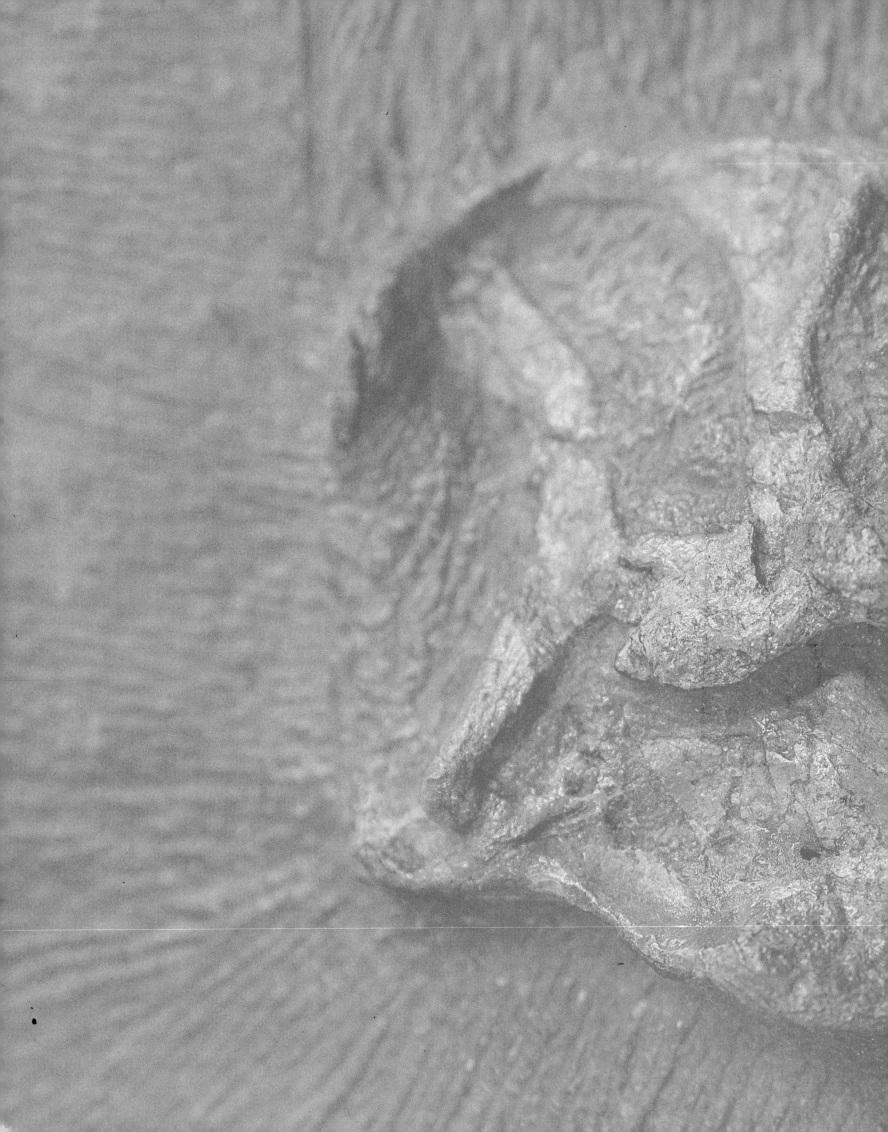